# The WAC Journal

Writing Across the Curriculum
Volume 32
2021

© 2022 Clemson University
Printed on acid-free paper in the USA
ISSN: 1544-4929

## Editors

Cameron Bushnell, Clemson University
David Blakesley, Clemson University

## Managing Editor

Allison Daniel, Clemson University

## Editorial Board

Heather Bastian, UNC Charlotte
Kristine Blair, Duquesne University
Jacob S. Blumner, U of Michigan, Flint
Heather Falconer, U of Maine, Orono
Jeffrey Galin, Florida Atlantic University
Xiqiao Wang, University of Pittsburgh
Joanna Wolfe, Carnegie Mellon University
Terry Myers Zawacki, George Mason University

## Review board

William P. Banks, East Carolina University
Christopher Basgier, Auburn University
Jessica Jorgenson Borchert, Pittsburg State U
Lauren Brentnell, U of Northern Colorado
Amy Cicchino, Auburn University
Geoffrey Clegg, Midwestern State University
Anthony DeGenaro, University of Detroit Mercy
Rasha Diab, University of Texas at Austin
John Eliason, Gonzaga University
Crystal N. Fodrey, Moravian University
Traci Gardner, Virginia Tech University
Analeigh Horton, University of Arizona
Bradley Hughes, University of Wisconsin
Liz Hutter, University of Dayton
Anna Knutson, Duquesne University
Michelle LaFrance, George Mason University
Sean Morey, U of Tennessee, Knoxville
Savannah Paige Murray, Appalachian State U
Lee Nickoson, Bowling Green State University
Sarah Peterson Pittock, Stanford University
Rebecca Pope-Ruark, Elon University
Jenna Pack Sheffield, University of New Haven
Douglas Walls, North Carolina State U
Carrie Wastal, U of California, San Diego
Travis Webster, Virginia Tech University

## Subscription Information

*The WAC Journal*
Parlor Press
3015 Brackenberry Drive
Anderson SC 29621
wacjournal@parlorpress.com
parlorpress.com/products/wac-journal
**Rates**: 1 year: $25; 3 years: $65; 5 years: $95.

## Submissions

*The WAC Journal* invites article submissions. The longest-running national peer-reviewed journal dedicated to writing across the curriculum, *The WAC Journal* seeks scholarly work at the intersection of writing with teaching, curriculum, learning, and research. Our review board welcomes inquiries, proposals, and articles from 3,000 to 6,000 words. We are especially interested in contributions that creatively approach a diverse range of anti-racist pedagogies, feminist rhetorics across the curriculum, intersectional contexts of feminism, and international WAC initiatives. Articles focusing on the ways WAC can be fostered in online courses are welcome as well. *The WAC Journal* supports a variety of diverse approaches to, and discussions of, writing across the curriculum. We welcome submissions from all WAC scholars that focus on writing across the curriculum, including topics on WAC program strategies, techniques and applications; emergent technologies and digital literacies across the curriculum; and WID. *The WAC Journal* is an open-access journal published annually by Clemson University, Parlor Press, and the WAC Clearinghouse. It is available by subscription in print through Parlor Press at https://parlorpress.com/products/wac-journal and online in open-access format at the WAC Clearinghouse via https://wac.colostate.edu/journal/. Articles are accepted throughout the year on a rolling basis. The peer review process is double-blind, which means all identifying information must be removed from the submission. Any submission notes must be included in the field provided for them, not in a separate cover letter or attachment. Submissions that aren't ready for double-blind review will be returned.

## Subscriptions

*The WAC Journal* is published annually in print by Parlor Press and Clemson University. Digital copies of the journal are simultaneously published at The WAC Clearinghouse in PDF format for free download. Print subscriptions support the ongoing publication of the journal and make it possible to offer digital copies as open access. Subscription rates: One year: $25; Three years: $65; Five years: $95. You can subscribe to The WAC Journal and pay securely by credit card or PayPal at the Parlor Press website: https://parlorpress.com/products/wac-journal. Or you can send your name, email address, and mailing address along with a check (payable to Parlor Press) to Parlor Press, 3015 Brackenberry Drive, Anderson SC 29621. Email: sales@parlorpress.com.

Reproduction of material from this publication, with acknowledgement of the source, is hereby authorized for educational use in nonprofit organizations.

# The WAC Journal
Volume 32, 2021

# Contents

From the Editors — 7

**PLENARY ADDRESS**

WAC Fearlessness, Sustainability, and Adaptability: Part One — 8
Chris Thaiss

**PLENARY ADDRESS**

Fearlessness, Sustainability, and Adaptability via WAC in a Small School — 16
Carol Rutz

**ARTICLES**

Feminist Rhetorics in Writing Across the Curriculum:
Supporting Students as Agents of Change — 23
Letizia Guglielmo, Judson T. Kidd, and Dominique McPhearson

"A long-lasting positive experience" from a Short-term Commitment:
The Power of the WAC TA Fellow Role for Disciplinary TAs — 42
Elisabeth L. Miller and Kathleen Daly Weisse

**INTERVIEW**

Conversations in Process: Two Dynamic Program Builders Talk about Adapting
WAC for Trilingual Hong Kong — 63
Terry Myers Zawacki

**FLASHBACK ARTICLES**

They — 72
Amy Warenda

Translation, Transformation, and "Taking it Back":
Moving between Face-to-Face and Online Writing in the Disciplines — 78
Heidi Skurat Harris, Tawnya Lubbes, Nancy Knowles, and Jacob Harris

REVIEW 99

*Linguistic Justice on Campus: Pedagogy and Advocacy for Multilingual Students,* edited by Brooke R. Schreiber, Eunjeong Lee, Jennifer T. Johnson, and Norah Fahim

REVIEWED BY JUSTIN NICHOLES

Contributors 105

# From the Editors

We would like to take the opportunity of this issue to announce a few new developments for the *WAC Journal*.

First, we welcome new members to the editorial and review boards. Editorial Board: Kristine Blair, Heather Falconer, Jeffrey R. Galin, and Xiqiao Wang (Editorial Board). Review Board: Will Banks, Christopher Basgier, Lauren Brentnell, John Eliason, Crystal N. Fodrey, Bradley Hughes, Liz Hutter, Michelle LaFrance, Savannah Paige Murray, Sarah Pittock, Douglas M. Walls, and Travis Webster. We greatly appreciate their willingness to join the dedicated board members who have been with the journal longer. Thanks to all! You ensure the journal remains a vibrant voice in the discipline.

Second, we are introducing a new feature with our next issue—a special topic forum—for which we will invite a guest editor, who will help us determine the special topic and who will help us in selecting the articles for the forum. Our next issue (volume 33), then, will be hybrid. We will solicit submissions for both a regular topic section and for a special topic section, three to five articles for each section, producing what will amount to a double issue. The development of a hybrid issue has a further aim: the introduction of a second, free-standing issue each year, beginning in a year or two.

To assist us in that endeavor, and to help with the day-to-day operations of the journal in the meantime, we have brought on Allison Daniel as Managing Editor. You may have had the pleasure of working with her already as she has served as our copyeditor and has helped us in communication with board members. We look forward to her assistance with all the operations of the journal.

Thank you for reading and enjoying the journal!

—*David Blakesley and Cameron Bushnell*

*Plenary Address*

# WAC Fearlessness, Sustainability, and Adaptability: Part One

## CHRIS THAISS

Carol and I feel honored to have been asked to give the opening plenary address at this wonderful conference, which has been so long in the making and which has handled creatively the changes necessitated by our need to stay safe during the pandemic.[1] We offer our thanks to the inimitable Mike Palmquist and all the members of the team who have made this event possible.

Five Decades—Carol and I are giving this plenary not only because we can talk about the "early days" of WAC, but because both of our WAC-ky careers span the five decades from the 70s through the twenty teens. We can talk about the three WAC ideals of fearlessness, sustainability, and adaptability because we've lived them in our careers as teachers, writers, and program planners and administrators. Of course, we've been extremely fortunate to have had the opportunity to work for many years at our institutions, and to reach funded retirements that give us the freedom to reflect on those decades of WAC work—and to keep contributing to WAC, as we choose, while also going down new paths. We are very thankful for that every day.

### Fearlessness

Teaching well always requires fearlessness. It requires honesty, compassion, so many hours per week, and the will to ask tough questions of ourselves, our students, and those to whom we report. It calls for imagination, taking chances with new ideas, risking failure. WAC fearlessness has always meant breaking through the thick walls of the silos of academe: challenging the comfort of those who have grown complacent with their assumptions about students and their potential, assumptions about who can learn and who can't. WAC fearlessness challenges the complacent walls of disciplinary jargons and people's unwillingness to learn to speak a language, even create a language, that others can understand.

For those who want to build a WAC culture where they teach, fearlessness means having many awkward conversations with administrators and chairs already burdened by time and money woes; it means acknowledging our own ignorance of

---

1. Presented at the International Writing Across the Curriculum Conference, August 2, 2021.

others' expertise, and listening to and keep listening to, and learning from people across an institution whose views on students and the goals of education differ from our own. WAC fearlessness always means asking others to come out of their own comfort zones, even as we must do the same. And if you do WAC for many years, fearlessness means learning to look forward to yet another opportunity to address the same concerns and answer the same questions that people have been asking you all those years: Why can't my students write? Why doesn't the English department/writing program do its job? How can I add writing to my teaching when I have so much material to cover? We already fund composition courses—why do we need to fund WAC?

In my own life, as I look back on when I began to get these WAC-ky notions, in about 1975, when my young family and I were struggling at the poverty line, I can't really account for why I became so enamored of the idea that students should be writing—and learning through writing—in all their subjects, not just in the first-year composition course sections, like those that I had been hired part-time to teach at two young colleges in the DC area, George Mason University and Northern Virginia Community College. In fact, I liked this idea so much that I eschewed the path that was conventional for college English teachers in those days—teaching and writing about literature—in order to badger my colleagues and department chairs about this new thing, writing across the curriculum, that a handful of US and British scholars were writing about.

I guess you could call my stance "fearless," meaning I was too dumb and young to know that I should be afraid of dooming my career chances before I even knew I might have a career.

Nevertheless, those visionary scholars-teachers-writers who were conceptualizing writing and learning across the curriculum, people like James Britton and Nancy Martin in the UK and Janet Emig in the US, were so eloquent and persistent that they inspired a bunch of youngsters like me to put on a nervous air of confidence about, dammit, maybe making a career out of teaching writing, and maybe even writing articles about it, and maybe even cajoling faculty in other departments to take a hand in their own students' writing education. I remember a conversation with the English chair at George Mason in 1976 who was listening skeptically to my "plans," and saying sympathetically "well, I guess there might be a few places where you could make a career out of teaching composition," but clearly, he implied, not there or at any place he had heard of.

But what I'm not telling you yet is that I was abetted in my crazy ideas by a growing cluster of college, high school, and elementary school teachers across the United States who formed the nucleus of what was first called the Bay Area Writing Project in 1974, and then became the National Writing Project in 1977, when James Gray,

Mary Ann Smith, Carol Tateishi, and others were able to secure funding from the new US Department of Education to form new sites. By 1976, there were fourteen sites in six states, and that was just the beginning. I was so fortunate to be mentored at George Mason by Donald Gallehr, who founded the Writing Project site there in 1977, and who gave me the chance to work with him and thus meet and be inspired by the K-12 teachers who came to our first summer institute in 1978.

I cannot assert too strongly how that growing collective of teachers from across grade levels and states gave young people like me the courage to do the unthinkable: transgress those borders of school cultures and disciplines in order to learn from one another and then, audaciously, to begin building efforts in each of our schools to provide a home for other teachers who saw writing not as a barrier that only the few could scale, but as an avenue, a gift, for more students to learn and grow and succeed.

Figure 1. Photo of Ken Macrorie, visiting consultant to the NVWP and the WAC Program, 1980. In the background, that's me, second from left.

## Sustainability

Though the term "sustainability" was still years away from becoming a buzzword in economics, in systems design, and in WAC, thanks to Michelle Cox, Jeff Galin, and Dan Melzer, the idea of sustaining what we started in the 1970s was always foremost in the minds of those of us who were initiating WAC in the late 1970s and early 1980s. One key toward sustainability was having the National Writing Project network and thus the ongoing invitation to talk to other folks over the phone and at conferences (no internet yet, some of you might remember) about what they were doing.

Beginning in 1981, we also had the National WAC Network that a few of us founded and that held semiannual open meetings at both 4Cs and, until 1985, at NCTE. The idea for this network came out of the annual workshops of the National Writing Project that were always held the day before the NCTE fall convention.

A number of program newsletters also sprang up and, if we wanted to, we could get on those mailing lists. Starting in 1982, a number of article collections and books on WAC programs began to emerge. Bit by bit, a research literature began to grow.

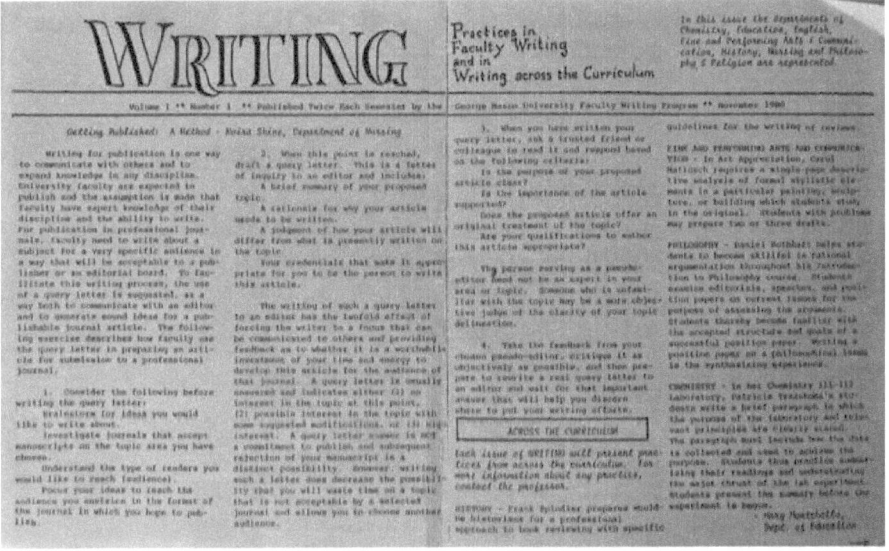

Figure 2. The very first issue of our newsletter from the GMU Faculty Writing Program, Nov. 1980.

The very fact of these new small networks gave people a big incentive to keep going despite the chronic problems with funding of any kind, the ongoing resistance of administrators and faculty, and being told regularly that there could be no future in this writing thing. I could talk on the phone with Barbara Walvoord at Loyola in

Baltimore or Toby Fulwiler and Art Young at Michigan Tech or Janet Emig in New Jersey or Elaine Maimon in Pennsylvania, and they would always be an inspiration.

Another sustainability tactic that emerged—and that we used at George Mason—was to group initiatives that had some goals in common. So the composition program, the small but growing writing center, the WAC workshops, and the Northern Virginia Writing Project, all still young, shared a joint leadership team. In key ways, the successes of each of these ventures depended on the success of them all, and vice versa. To cite one example, when we started WAC workshops for Mason faculty in 1978, we asked high school teacher consultants from the Writing Project to run some of the workshops, since they had greater expertise and on-the-job experience than anyone on our campus. Meanwhile, I was coordinating in-service courses for the Writing Project in local high schools and at the same time directing both the composition courses at Mason and its small writing center, which we first called the writing lab in 1976 and then the writing place later on, because the tutors and I thought it sounded cooler. Please remember, this was before there was a research literature on writing program design and management and years before there were graduate programs in writing studies, not to mention anything like independent writing programs for undergraduates.

This fully collaborative model worked fine to get each of these efforts going and build some credibility, enough to inspire other folks to want to join the teams and take on leadership—and to give the university admin enough confidence to fork over money for release time for the directors. (In 1979, I had one course release total for administering both comp and the writing center). But by 1985, six years in, each of the four entities had separate directors, all minimally compensated for their time, but all dedicated to growing each entity and collaborating with the others.

A third key component of sustainability, and maybe the most important, was the goal of bringing more and more people into leadership roles, whether as steering committee members, consultants, editors, contributing writers, or some other structure.

Figure 3. First anthology of in-house papers from the Northern Virginia Writing Project, 1979.

It's not a bad idea for directors to make it known that they'll only do a job for a certain length of time, so others will be thinking about continuity and the role that they might play in it. It also inspires the director to be cultivating successors and to encourage newer members of a team to develop and bring forward their own ideas. The organization is always more important than any one person. I've always thought that administratively it's dangerous to let anyone believe that an individual leader is indispensable. The myth of indispensability can lead directors to see others as rivals not as teammates, and it can lead to the death of the program once the leader, eventually and inevitably, steps aside.

## Adaptability

The third principle I'll discuss today is adaptability. I'll put it bluntly: There is no sustainability without adaptability. Times change, leading ideas change, finances change, technologies change, people change, access to opportunities change, climates change, and on and on. Writing has changed utterly from the 1970s to now, and there are departments and degrees and curricular initiatives now that would never have been imagined thirty or twenty or even ten years ago. So, of course, WAC has had to change. Sometimes the changes come quickly, and adaptation has to come quickly. In 1978, we ran the first WAC workshops. In 1980, we got a state grant to set up a Virginia state WAC network. In 1982, the whole Mason writing curriculum changed by dropping the second first-year writing course and adding required WID courses in the junior year, which we had to design. In 1984, first-year students could opt for an entirely cross-disciplinary curriculum, called PAGE—the Plan for Alternative General Education—which had total WAC, with no first-year writing course.

By the late 1980s, ten years into our program at Mason, email—which we could never have imagined in 1976—was everywhere, and even these things called websites, think of it, were beginning to be developed. In 1991, the faculty senate demanded writing intensive courses. And on and on.

In 1978, how silly we'd have been to imagine that we could know what a sustainable program was. Without the will to adapt, WAC, and no program, can keep going. Continually, the people invested in an idea must be alert for change, can even lead change, and must be ready to respond to change. Even just two years ago, who could have imagined how what we mean by writing and what we mean by teaching could have changed so much because of a virus? And even last year at this time, who could have imagined the ways teachers and students would have adapted to, much less foreseen, the social justice, political, and technological changes that have brought about new challenges for adaptation?

Just nine months ago, I was into my fourth year of busy retirement, four years removed from undergrad teaching, and one year removed from advising my last PhD student at UC Davis. Then I was asked to teach again my favorite undergrad course, writing in science, and to do so asynchronously online, for my first time ever, using the learning management system, Canvas, that UC Davis adopted just after I had retired. Fortunately, I could adapt and even love the challenge, but only because the writing program and the entire university had been so quick in adapting to the pandemic challenge and creating help services for "newbies" (so to speak) like me.

And if our teaching and program management have to be ready for change, so must our research. For example, the International WAC/WID Mapping Project, which began in 2005, revised survey-based research that Susan McLeod had begun with Susan Shirley back in 1987, and which she revised in 1997 with Eric Miraglia.

The survey design for US programs that PhD student Tara Porter and I announced in 2006 captured changes in WAC since 1997 that were now relevant in the first decade of the new millennium. But that research has gone on since, based on further changes in design, theory, and objectives. Here at IWAC, my Davis colleague Kendon Kurzer, with Katherine O'Meara, Greer Murphy, and Robyn Russo will be presenting on a new interactive re-envisioning of the mapping project research, which they have named the Writing Sites Project. Then, Michele Zugnoni of Northwestern will present current results of the latest iteration of the US WAC survey, which began in 2015 and which continues to accept survey responses today. These iterations of this research are described on the WAC/WID Mapping Project website, mappingproject.ucdavis.edu.

So, in closing: Those of us who have given years to WAC have to be always thinking what of any paradigm is worth holding onto and what of the new can be adopted and adapted. If we don't adapt, fearlessly and we hope sustainably, we might find ourselves, oh I don't know, denying climate change, and maybe even thinking that retirement means not continuing to work creatively. But if we accept the challenge to adapt, who knows what adventures and new ideas await WAC and its fearless leaders.

Thanks to all of you for being present and for the fearless work you do.

## References

Cox, Michelle, Jeffrey Galin, and Dan Melzer (2018). *Sustainable WAC: A Whole Systems Approach to Launching and Developing Writing Across the Curriculum Programs.* National Council of Teachers of English.

Gray, James and Richard Sterling (2005). *Teachers at the Center: A Memoir of the Early Years of the National Writing Project.* National Writing Project.

The International WAC/WID Mapping Project. Accessible 2021: http://mappingproject.ucdavis.edu .

McLeod, Susan, and Susan Shirley (1987). "Appendix: National Survey of Writing Across the Curriculum Programs." *Strengthening Programs for Writing Across the Curriculum.* Susan McLeod, ed. San Francisco: Jossey Bass.

McLeod, Susan and Eric Miraglia (1997). "Whither WAC? Interpreting the Stories/Histories of Mature WAC Programs." *WPA: Writing Program Administration,* 20:3, 46–65.

Thaiss, Chris and Tara Porter (2010). "The State of WAC/WID in 2010: Methods and Results of the U.S. Survey of the International WAC/WID Mapping Project," *College Composition and Communication,* 61:3 (February 2010), 534–70.

*Plenary Address*

# Fearlessness, Sustainability, and Adaptability via WAC in a Small School

## CAROL RUTZ

I am honored to be paired with Chris Thaiss for this plenary address, and I look forward to attempting to field questions.[1] As you have just heard, Chris presents a marvelous, longitudinal view of WAC from the perspective of an early and ongoing participant. I will say up front that Chris grants me a longer tenure as a WAC scholar than I deserve; while he was indeed doing WAC in the 1970s, WAC was a feature at Carleton College at that time—but well before I was on the scene. The story I offer is more of a case study of a place that stumbled into WAC for local reasons and has since taken on some status as an early adopter. As much as our field, rhetoric and composition, has striven to establish itself as a full member of the humanities, writ large, our history is spotty. This summer's conference provides a chance to dip into the history of WAC as well as its current manifestations, mindful of the protean nature of the beast illustrated by three key terms we have agreed to feature: fearlessness, sustainability, and adaptability.

## Fearlessness

Harriet Sheridan's story of "Teaching Writing Extra-Territorially" provides an ideal example for our rubric of fearlessness. (See her 1979 piece in *ADE*.) Harriet Sheridan had been a fixture in Carleton's English department for many years when she was promoted to dean of the college during the presidency of Howard Swearer. Later, after Swearer assumed the presidency at Brown University and Sheridan had served as Carleton's interim president for a year, Sheridan followed him to Brown. The Sheridan Center for Teaching and Learning is named in her honor. She was a powerhouse.

---

1. Presented at the International Writing Across the Curriculum Conference, July 31, 2021. Revised slightly for publication in the *WAC Journal*.

Figure 1. Photo of Harriet Sheridan courtesy of the Carleton Archives

Back to Carleton in the 1970s. The college's catalog listed a writing requirement for graduation at least since 1960. The requirement began as a two-course sequence, was shortened over the years to one course, and, eventually, to a five-week course—half of one of Carleton's ten-week terms. Sheridan was in a position to observe these transitions as well as participate in them as an instructor, department chair, and dean. She faced irrefutable data showing that the courses, even the five-week version, were not particularly appreciated by students or faculty. Students complained bitterly about the courses, and finding faculty to teach them became increasingly difficult.

Nevertheless, college-wide, faculty expected high quality student writing, and where students did not meet a professor's standard, writing instruction from the English department was clearly at fault. (This complaint, in some form, probably dates to the ancient Greeks.) Recognizing that writing *instruction* differed from the *assigning* of writing, Sheridan decided to initiate a reform designed to 1) take some pressure off the English department; 2) spread responsibility for writing instruction to faculty in other departments; and 3) mobilize the writing skills of selected senior students to serve as rhetoric assistants to the participating faculty in departments other than English.

To get this innovation off the ground, Sheridan organized a two-week rhetoric institute in the summer of 1975 for the first set of faculty who agreed to include writing instruction as well as delivering their usual disciplinary material. Readings for that early faculty workshop included Aristotle's *Rhetoric*, as well as an exercise in norming grades for student work. Next, faculty writing was subjected to the same treatment, which resulted in an assignment for them: an essay describing their learning about how to teach writing based on what they could expect of students and how their own writing fared upon close examination.

To support this curricular experiment, the Educational Policy Committee's minutes (2/4/1975) include this resolution:

> Resolved: that at all course levels, where appropriate, all members of the Carleton faculty should require term papers and other written work of their students. We do not think it appropriate that at an institution such as Carleton such written work should be returned to the students with little or no evaluation beyond a letter grade. Therefore we further resolve that, as a matter of policy, written work be returned with detailed commentary by way of evaluation not only of the accuracy of the content of the paper but of its form. As part of the evaluation of the effectiveness of written work in all courses, errors of spelling, grammar and style should be explicitly noted.
>
> In order to establish common bases for judging writing skill and providing guidance for improvement, summer Rhetoric Institutes should be arranged annually to include interested faculty from all disciplines and student rhetoric assistants, until it is determined (by the Dean of the College) that they are no longer needed. Although for the present the object is to increase the options for fulfilling the writing requirement, **in the long run the goal is a continuing college-wide involvement in developing all students' writing skills**.

Despite the current-traditional language in that resolution, the intended goal was to spread the responsibility for writing instruction across the college via dedicated instruction in all departments.

When the program was launched, about half a dozen faculty agreed to design extra writing experiences for a subset of students in designated courses. A student rhetoric assistant worked with each faculty member to facilitate the writing goals of the course for those students attempting to satisfy the graduation requirement through the course. The final decision, separated from the grade in the course, was an up-or-down decision on the part of the professor.

## Sustainability

This system, with minor changes, persisted for about twenty-five years. Elaine Maimon, who knew Sheridan, notes in her chapter in Fulwiler and Young (1990), that Sheridan simultaneously invented the faculty workshop, what we now call WAC, and also fielded the notion of a writing center that would employ peer tutors. Sheridan deserves that credit and more. After her departure, the English department continued to provide stand-alone courses in writing, and the "extra-territorial" courses expanded beyond the humanities to include introductory courses in the sciences and social sciences.

Eventually, though, as Thomas Kuhn might predict, the paradigm wore thin. Students learned via the grapevine which professors were likely to award "WR" and which to avoid. Faculty continued to complain about student writing, no matter who was teaching it. In 1996, a faculty task force examined the problem and produced a report that noted that, in contrast to the homogeneous student body of 1975, growing diversity among students presented a serious concern, with faculty confessing to their own shortcomings when encountering dialect or ESL features in student writing. Writing instruction, never a straightforward matter, now seemed deficient for cultural reasons.

Even though not one example of student writing was read and evaluated, the report's recommendations were rather far-reaching. In addition to hiring and supporting qualified ESL staff, there was the notion of a portfolio system that students would keep with them, adding written material throughout their four years. However, the mechanics of collecting and evaluating such an artifact were considered beyond the capacity of the college to manage at that time.

## Adaptability

Change arrived in the form of new personnel and new pedagogy.

A little personal biography: I worked on the Carleton staff for ten years in a variety of jobs, leaving in the fall of 1992 to pursue a doctorate in English with a rhetoric and composition emphasis at the University of Minnesota. In 1997, to my great surprise, I was hired back as an ABD for a one-year, half-time job in faculty development for writing. I had an office, a nice computer, and a door I could close to work on my dissertation when I wasn't working with former colleagues—and those who had arrived over the previous five years—on WAC. I quickly learned that the Sheridan program that featured a subset of students attempting writing requirement in a range of disciplinary courses was a matter of faculty habit but not a healthy pedagogy.

The 1996 review of writing had surfaced problems but few solutions. Fewer faculty were willing to put in extra effort for the WR students in their courses, and those who were willing to provide the assignments often requested specific senior students as writing assistants as a means of reducing their own effort for commentary or conferences to address writing problems.

Shortly after I arrived and began to understand faculty worries about writing, Carleton was invited to submit a grant application to a St. Paul-based foundation that had supported us before, most notably for our learning and teaching center back in 1992 (very early for a small school). The grant was for faculty development, and my supervisor, an associate dean, and I decided to improve programming for faculty in WAC. The preliminary proposal was deemed interesting by the site visitors, but they complained that we did not include any assessment. Gulp.

So *fearlessly* feeling our way toward a diktat we did not completely understand, we decided to make writing assessment the center of the proposal, launching our sophomore portfolio as a means of faculty development supported by visiting speakers, workshops, support for conference attendance, summer funding for revising or creating WAC courses, and reading the portfolios themselves. My boss and I intuitively understood how this kind of assessment would be meaningful and even fun for our colleagues. We suspected that faculty would initially balk at reading student work they had not assigned and was outside their areas of expertise, and we hoped that cautiousness would lead to curiosity about how writing could be successful in a variety of forms and disciplinary contexts. We were right.

One feature of the grant that turned out to be essential involved senior faculty in promoting the assessment project. An investment in course releases for professors of classics, economics, and astrophysics paid off handsomely as these colleagues recruited others to participate in various ways—including getting the new assessment program approved by the faculty as a whole.

The initial three-year grant was renewed for a total of six years. With a focus on new faculty as well as anyone else interested, one can do a lot of WAC-related damage over six years! Whatever I know about assessment started with *doing* it; formal learning through the literature, conferences, and so on came later.

Remembering that WAC as introduced at Carleton by Harriet Sheridan began as a faculty development activity, we were able to add assessment to her insight that writing *instruction* differs from *assigning* writing. As the portfolio recipe was *adapted* with ample faculty input, the assessment instrument itself spoke to a shared goal of promoting communication within and among discourse communities. Furthermore, the interdisciplinary design of the portfolio brought that same goal to the attention of students in an unavoidable way. No student could just submit her favorite papers; she had to show breadth of material as well as form.

Regarding *sustainability*, the portfolio assessment began as a pilot in 2004 and continues today, outlasting my tenure as director and prospering under a new director who has ably coped with the challenges of the pandemic by shifting the reading and scoring processes online. The faculty development benefit of reading work that a) one has not assigned and b) ranges beyond one's disciplinary expertise continues.

Many of us will recall Ed White's frequent caution that WAC is subject to cycles that depend on leadership, budget, curricular fads, and so forth. My experience at Carleton and as a consultant to a range of other colleges and universities points me toward a different metaphor. I see WAC as more of a sine curve that fluctuates according to various influences. As a WAC leader, my job is to keep the amplitude up, to anticipate the dips and offer support as needed.

As I have worked with many campuses on WAC, I have learned that size matters. Therefore, I want to briefly address the difference among community colleges (where about half of the college-level writing courses are taught), universities (where writing instructors earn credentials), and small liberal arts colleges, where WAC often thrives.

Carleton is a dinky little place in Northfield, Minnesota, with about 2,000 students and about 280 full and part-time faculty. (Northfield is also home to St. Olaf College across the Cannon River, which serves over 3,000 students.) Small schools tend to engender fierce loyalty among their alumni, faculty, and staff. Although the small-school percentage of higher education offerings nationally is around five percent and declining, small schools foster achievement, promote their graduates, and, to a considerable degree, populate their boards with plenty of alumni. Details differ from school to school, of course. Until fairly recently, however, as consortia and other combinations have developed to address issues in common, small school administrations were loath to reach out to peers for ideas, data, or other information. Even with an early WAC program, Carleton was no different: a report naming problems with student writing did not engender an SOS to any outside institution.

I well remember a gathering convened by the Teagle Foundation during an AAC&U convention early in this century, where grants were being offered to small schools—with the requirement to partner with at least one other institution to address some mutual assessment effort. The attendees had many questions, and a few administrators showed interest in collaboration with other schools. In a dramatic counter to the Teagle agenda, a dean of a small school in the Northeast categorically denounced the value of combining personnel and data, arguing that sharing data was dangerous to that or any institution's well-being. A hush followed that outburst. (Parenthetically, invitations from Teagle and other foundations accomplished good work with partnerships among small schools all over the country. Carleton participated in at least three.)

Back to the outburst: To be fair, that dean was speaking out of a moment similar to Harriet Sheridan's approach to tackling the writing curriculum at Carleton in the 1970s. Sheridan did not care about writing at other schools; she did not pick up the phone to ask for advice; she assumed that the Carleton environment was *sui generis*; therefore, she proceeded with institutional legislation and a whole lot of arm twisting.

From what I have observed as a consultant to about thirty small schools, defensiveness persists in some quarters, yet more faculty and administrators seem increasingly open to collaborative ideas that are well supported in the literature and in practice. This is a healthy shift, and it augurs well for WAC overall. As I have reviewed the program for this conference, I see just a handful of folks from small schools. The virtual format may be the main reason, which is understandable. I do hope that virtual access brings in plenty of attendees from small school WAC programs. There is great work going on and more work to be done.

## Works Cited

Carleton College. Minutes of the Educational Policy Committee, February 4, 1975.
Sheridan, Harriet. "Teaching Writing Extra-Territorially," *ADE Bulletin*, vol. 44, 1979.
Fulwiler, Toby, and Art Young. *Programs That Work*, Heinemann, 1990.

*Articles*

# Feminist Rhetorics in Writing Across the Curriculum: Supporting Students as Agents of Change

LETIZIA GUGLIELMO, JUDSON T. KIDD, AND
DOMINIQUE MCPHEARSON

Feminist rhetorical theories and practices, applied across disciplines, have the potential to shape students' writing and research processes and to support the goals of writing across the curriculum. When deliberately guiding course design and writing to learn (WTL) activities, feminist rhetorics and pedagogical practices foster collaboration and co-construction of knowledge, and they can begin to decenter authority and disrupt hierarchy, centering student voices and amplifying marginalized perspectives. Feminist rhetorical theories and practices not only support the goals of writing to engage (WTE) activities, but also extend their goals, inviting students to join and to contribute to conversations in ways that actively diversify, reshape, and disrupt dominant narratives and meaning-making practices within those disciplines and professions, and facilitating students' engagement in change agency. Guided by a collaborative ethos, this article provides a multivocal exploration and reflection on the authors' experiences as students and instructor to both perform and to theorize feminist rhetorics and to demonstrate how individual positionalities and disciplinary expertise informed and were shaped by course content, ultimately supporting the authors' work as change agents across disciplines.

---

## Introduction

In her foreword to *Diverse Approaches to Teaching, Learning, and Writing Across the Curriculum: IWAC at 25,* Mya Poe (2020) reminds us, "WAC is about people making texts together, not studying texts in isolation, and forming meaningful collaborations has long been central to successful WAC programs" (p. xiii). Later in their introduction, the collection's editors argue, "Collaborative ethos and the drive to integrate diverse approaches, perspectives, and expertise remain the backbone of the

WAC movement, our enduring point of connection" (Bartlett et al., 2020, p. 7). With similar goals in "integrat[ing] diverse approaches, perspectives, and expertise," feminist rhetorical and pedagogical practices value collaboration in facilitating a decentering of authority and the inclusion of multiple voices and lived experiences as an active and ongoing process of meaning-making. Significantly, "this increasingly diverse range of work is not being done by women professionals alone, or only by scholars who label themselves as operating within feminist rhetorical studies, or even by single scholars" (Royster & Kirsch, 2012, p. 43).

This article grows out of an online interdisciplinary writing intensive course (WIC) on feminist rhetorics offered during the spring 2021 semester. As both a cross-leveled (undergraduate and graduate) and cross-listed section with three distinct prefixes, the course enrolled students across seven departments and multiple programs, including graduate students in American studies, professional writing, and secondary and middle grades education, and undergraduate students in English, interdisciplinary studies, philosophy, and technical communication and interactive design. At the conclusion of our course, and with new knowledge gleaned from our exploration of feminist rhetorics, we found ourselves asking how we can engage and apply feminist rhetorics in spaces outside of a feminist rhetorics course, spaces that allow us to underscore foundations of feminist rhetorical theories and practices as part of broader writing and research processes. This question prompted our continued collaboration, reflection on course assignments and activities, and work on this article. We extended the collective writing and meaning-making we'd engaged in during the semester with both individual reflections on our course experience and the final project, and pre-writing via email developed by guiding questions. In online virtual meetings, we identified points of connection in this initial self-reflection and writing and began to articulate how feminist rhetorical theories and practices had allowed us to make meaning and connections with disciplinary expertise and to envision the applications of these practices in a variety of rhetorical spaces.

In the sections that follow, we engage in a multivocal exploration and reflection on our experiences to both perform and to theorize feminist rhetorics and their potential in underscoring the goals of writing across the curriculum (WAC). Guided by and engaging with a robust scholarly tradition on the role of writing to learn activities (WTL) within WAC, we explore how feminist rhetorics and pedagogies both contribute to and extend the broader goals of WTL, including meaning-making writing tasks and deep approaches to learning (see Anderson et al., 2015; Gere et al., 2019) and support the higher-order activities that Palmquist (2020) has more recently termed Writing to Engage (WTE). According to Palmquist (2020),

> As a part of a larger conceptual framework for the design of writing activities and assignments in WAC courses, the use of this concept [writing to

engage] increases the nuance and precision with which we can discuss the relationship between writing and critical thinking as well as the role that writing can play in helping students advance in their disciplines and professions. (p. 17)

We extend Palmquist's (2020) argument to demonstrate how feminist rhetorical theories and practices not only support the goals of WTE activities, but also extend their goals, inviting students to join and to contribute to conversations in ways that actively diversify, reshape, and disrupt dominant narratives and meaning-making practices within those disciplines and professions, and facilitating students' engagement in change agency. Essential to these processes we argue, are collaboration and opportunities for communal, collective meaning-making.

## Feminisms Across the Curriculum

Although our course focus on feminist rhetorical theory and practice required engagement with a number of foundational texts, including primary and secondary sources that continue to circulate in current conversations in the field, for the purposes of this article we point to a few key texts that have broad application across disciplines, contributing to the aims of WTL and WTE pedagogies and shaping the work of writers and researchers in engaging diverse perspectives. These foundational theories and practices may serve WAC practitioners and scholars in a variety of courses without the requirement that course content shift exclusively to a study of rhetoric. Broadly, feminist scholars have engaged rhetorical theory and practice from a number of angles, including expanding the traditional rhetorical canon to include women and other marginalized rhetors; expanding the scope and location of rhetoric, including challenging what counts as rhetorical theory, practice, and space; questioning who gets to speak, when, where, and to or for whom; and actively listening for silences and erasures and recovering or centering those voices, perspectives, and lived experiences (see Royster & Kirsch, 2012; Buchanan & Ryan, 2010; Ede et al., 1995; Foss et al., 1999; Reynolds, 1993). Central to these theories and practices are new methodologies and methods for conducting research and ways of understanding feminist rhetorics as embodied and performed (Royster & Kirsch, 2012). In the WAC classroom, feminist rhetorics also inform, and may be supported by, feminist pedagogical strategies that shape WTL and WTE pedagogies.

In her 1987 article, "What Is Feminist Pedagogy?" Carolyn M. Shrewsbury explains,

> Feminist pedagogy is engaged teaching/learning—engaged with self in a continuing reflective process; engaged actively with the material being studied; engaged with others in a struggle to get beyond our sexism and racism

and classism and homophobia and other destructive hatreds and to work together to enhance our knowledge; engaged with the community, with traditional organizations, and with movements for social change. (p. 6)

In the last three decades, women's studies teacher-scholars and those outside the discipline have continued to engage, to expand, and to apply in a growing number of contexts the liberatory, decentered, and activist potential of feminist pedagogical strategies and theories (see Crabtree et al.Licona, 2009; Byrne, 2000). In teaching and learning environments guided by feminist pedagogy, students take more active roles in and responsibility for their own and their peers' learning, guided by reflective engagement with each other and with course content, and they identify opportunities for applying that learning outside of classroom settings. Feminist pedagogy is often supported by collaborative classroom practices and feminist rhetorical strategies like intervention and interruption that highlight and amplify marginalized voices and perspectives (Reynolds, 1998; Rinehart, 2002; Ryan, 2006; Guglielmo, 2012). Exploring the intersections of feminist pedagogy and online learning, Chick and Hassel (2009) claim, "Within this community, students care about others' learning and well-being as well as their own, and they feel free to use their sites of authority—where they already stand and what they already know—to help contribute to the knowledge of the course" (p. 198)

In their groundbreaking text *Transforming Scholarship: Why Women's and Gender Studies Students are Changing Themselves and the World*, Michele Tracy Berger and Cheryl Radeloff (2011) argue that "students pursuing questions in women's and gender studies are part of an emerging vanguard of knowledge producers in the US and globally . . . trained to consider how their efforts in the classroom can be translated to affect the status of women and men (and anyone outside the gender binary) beyond the borders of their college or university" (p. 5). Graduates who enter professional fields with gender studies coursework are better positioned to foster diversity, equity, and inclusivity in the workplace and in their communities (Colatrella, 2014). In addition to the language and strategies Berger and Radeloff (2011) provide students to apply their classroom learning outside of classroom contexts, they invite students to identify as "change agents," which they define as including "a commitment to public engagement beyond the borders of the academic classroom" (p. 25).

Centering these theories and practices, we engaged feminist rhetorics and pedagogies in a variety of ways throughout the semester as part of our online writing activities and meaning-making practices. As we'll discuss in later sections, feminist rhetorics facilitated our collective use of feminist intervention and discursive interruption and allowed us to remain mindful of how and when we were centering specific voices and perspectives and particular rhetorical practices and sites. In terms of research, feminist rhetorics informed research across disciplines, allowing us to engage with disciplinary expertise and knowledge in new ways. As a research methodology, feminist rhetorics allowed us to ask new and different questions across disciplines and to find multiple ways into this work. Finally, as a pedagogical strategy guiding our writing and research activities, feminist rhetorical theories and practices facilitated the co-construction of knowledge—collaborative meaning-making—in the online course, shaping our understanding of the potential and possibilities for feminist rhetorical practices outside of our (virtual) classroom space. In guiding WTL activities and the final project for the course, feminist rhetorics became a strategy for intersectional activism and engagement and for advancing our individual and collective understanding of change agency.

## Critical Imagination, Strategic Contemplation, and Self-Rhetoric

In their landmark text *Feminist Rhetorical Practices: New Horizons for Rhetoric, Composition, and Literacy Studies,* Jacqueline Jones Royster and Gesa E. Kirsch (2012) introduce "four critical tasks" that both map and expand the terrain and scope of feminist rhetorical theory and practice and provide a framework for future work (p. 13). Within this framework are two concepts that became central to our course and to shaping our WTL and WTE activities: critical imagination and strategic contemplation. As an "inquiry tool," critical imagination invites "seeing the noticed and the unnoticed, rethinking what is there and not there, and speculating about what could be there instead" (Royster & Kirsch, 2012, p. 20). This process, Royster and Kirsch (2012) explain, facilitates "the possibility of rescue, recovery, and (re)inscription while bringing attention to the challenge of expanding knowledge and re-forming not only what constitutes knowledge but also whether and how we value and accredit it" (p. 20). Closely connected to critical imagination, strategic contemplation constitutes a "consciously enacted contemplative process" that allows us to "pay attention to how lived experiences shape our perspectives" and to consider how "an ethos of humility, respect, and care [can] shape our research" (Royster & Kirsch, 2012, p. 22). In practice, this work requires deep reflection and listening, including learning to identify silences, omissions, and erasures and the reinforcement of dominant narratives.

Combined with critical imagination and strategic contemplation, and certainly informed by these practices, Kimberly Harrison's (2003) exploration of self-rhetoric and ethos in Southern U.S. women's civil war diaries provided us with a third critical concept for our work:

> Self-rhetoric . . . posit[s] the self as a site for rhetorical negotiation of competing ideologies and material conditions that allow for possibilities and limitations of self-definition and presentation. The term implies the personal

> rhetorical negotiations that then result in the public presentation of self. . . . In constructing one's sense of self in response to social, cultural, and material forces, the rhetor relies on self-persuasion to internalize and reconcile new and perhaps conflicting views of identity. (p. 244)

As we will explore in greater detail in later sections of this article, it was not only Harrison's (2003) definition of self-rhetoric that became significant to our work, but also her focus on diaries as a rhetorical space and on the rhetorical activities of confederate women, a subject that allowed us to apply strategic contemplation and discursive intervention in our reading and discussion of the text to highlight the silencing and erasure of Black voices and, particularly, of Black women's voices.

Together these texts and three concepts made salient how feminist rhetorics can become significant across disciplines even if the focus of the course is not rhetorical. We engage in rhetorical practices regularly across disciplines, even if we are not identifying those practices as rhetorical, and these rhetorical acts facilitate telling our stories and sharing our perspectives and listening to or looking for the stories and perspectives of others. Also significant in our work together was a recognition that rhetoric was not simply an academic pursuit but a way for women and other marginalized people to survive and fight for change. In their application, these concepts significantly shaped WTL activities throughout our course, activities that allowed us "to use writing as a tool for learning rather than a test of that learning, to . . . explain concepts or ideas to [our]selves, to ask questions, to make connections, to speculate, to engage in critical thinking" (McLeod & Maimon, 2000, p. 579). Shaping these connections and this critical thinking as part of writing to engage activities "well suited to encouraging the use of cognitive skills such as reflecting, applying, analyzing, and evaluating, skills that are valuable for grappling with the information, ideas, and arguments within a discipline," (Palmquist, 2020, p. 12), as part of our writing and research, these three concepts helped us to know what questions to ask, where to look for information, what to look for in those sources, and how to identify who and what was missing. We came to understand the significance of rhetorical position in research and how and when to ask questions about voice, perspective, experience, visibility, silencing, and erasure. As we illustrate in the following section, WTL activities grounded by feminist rhetorics and those that guide research and writing processes can help students to diversify their research topics and resources and to engage in active and communal meaning-making.

### Reflections and Connections: Feminist Rhetorics in Theory and Practice

In this section we explore—individually and collectively—how we put theory into practice throughout the semester and how course content and our collaborative engagement shaped our learning, writing, and research. In order to highlight and to amplify our individual voices and experiences at key moments, and to provide a diversity of perspectives, we self-identify by first names to demonstrate the extent to which feminist rhetorics facilitated a variety of connections and ways in that were at once interdisciplinary and individual. Furthermore, we demonstrate how individual positionalities and disciplinary expertise informed and were shaped by an interdisciplinary and intersectional approach to course content, ultimately supporting our work as change agents across disciplines. We identify WTL and WTE activities as sites for not only discussing, theorizing, and exploring but also applying feminist rhetorics. Furthermore, we find collaborative inquiry as essential to this process, both in our meaning-making within the course and in extending this meaning-making outside of the immediate course context.

*Letizia*

As a significant part of my teaching and scholarship, feminist rhetorics have both informed my professional work and helped me give voice to my experience as a cisgender woman and child of immigrants grappling with liminal and contested spaces (see Daniell & Guglielmo, 2016; Guglielmo, 2019). Although I had previously taught graduate and undergraduate courses in both writing and rhetoric and in gender and women's studies that included texts in feminist rhetoric and that were grounded in feminist pedagogical practices, this course offered a unique opportunity to center these theories and practices with students and to engage them through inter- and multidisciplinary lenses. Both guided by and embodying the interdisciplinary nature of feminist rhetorics, this course was designed to introduce students to feminist rhetorical theory and practice, to draw students into ongoing scholarly conversations on feminist rhetorics, and to prompt them to begin contributing to those conversations in ways that were meaningful and relevant for their ongoing academic and professional work across disciplines. From low-stakes writing assignments to the final project, students were invited, "to connect on a personal level, to find meaning beyond the specifics of the assignment itself, and to imagine future selves or future writing identities connected to their goals and interests" (Eodice et al., 2017). According to Palmquist (2020) this meaningful connection is essential to the critical thinking required of WTE activities (p. 15).

From the outset of the course, I designed module introductions and overviews to support students' engagement with course readings and module content with two general goals in mind: modeling the kinds of questions that could grow out of and be shaped by feminist rhetorical theory and practice and demonstrating that our learning was in process and co-constructed, subject to revision, expansion, and deliberation. For example, during module one, I asked:

- What does it mean for the work of feminist rhetorics or feminist rhetoricians to be interdisciplinary? What are the benefits of interdisciplinarity?
- What role do silence, reflection, embodiment, and "linger[ing] deliberately" play in feminist research and in feminist rhetoric? (Royster & Kirsch, 2012, p. x)
- What *is* feminist rhetoric and where do we find feminist rhetorics or feminist rhetors?

We would return to or expand the scope of many of these questions during each subsequent module, and online writing and discussion activities were designed to allow us to reflect on, deliberate, and reconsider and refine responses, reinforcing the collective and fluid nature of our learning (e.g., How does this reading shape your understanding of rhetoric? Of feminist rhetorics? Of what counts as a rhetorical space? Of what counts as feminist rhetorical practice or feminist rhetorical activities?)

Given our online format, reflection on these questions as part of our collaborative meaning-making was facilitated during each module by our learning management system's (LMS) online discussion board. According to Mays Imad (2021), "Meaning-making gives us a sense of control and increases our sense of belonging, self-worth, and personal fulfillment. At the same time, it also helps us feel as if we are a part of something bigger than ourselves" (p. 8). Although I typically posted questions in the module overview similar to those included above to guide reading and analysis, students were invited to find their own ways into the discussion by drawing on those questions and posing questions of their own (see sample questions embedded in the bulleted list). In addition to initiating their own and responding to one another's posts, the act of reading each other's reflections and analyses and considering peers' questions offered opportunities for continuing to engage in critical imagination and strategic contemplation, as subsequent sections of this article will illustrate. Within online courses, discussion board activities "provide a timely opportunity to build collaborative bridges between professors and students, with an objective of sharing power and innovating feminist praxis on both sides" (Turpin, 2007, p. 19). Online discussion boards can serve as the center of writing and reflection activities in online courses, and those digital spaces have the potential to invite increased participation and to facilitate a variety of feminist rhetorical activities (see Chick & Hassel, 2009; Guglielmo, 2012; Guglielmo, 2009).

Fulfilling different purposes over the course of the semester as part of our writing and research processes, discussion activities were often public and sometimes private, facilitating a variety of WTL and WTE activities. In addition to space for reflection, these posts also offered space for low-stakes prewriting activities for longer writing assignments and for sharing what we already knew or didn't know about rhetoric and feminist rhetorics at the start of the semester and revisiting that knowledge at mid-semester. In addition to the questions shared above, at mid-semester I asked students for a more cumulative reflection on their engagement with feminist rhetorics, thinking about their own way into the work and about opportunities to extend, contribute to, or complicate the conversations we'd been tracing on feminist rhetorics as they looked ahead to future work and the final project for the course.

As a deliberate strategy to decenter my own voice in this online space and to reinforce the co-constructed meaning and collective knowledge among the group, I rarely responded directly to posts on the discussion board and at the start of each week's module overview, I began with a reflection on the previous discussion activity, centering students' voices (each by name) and the connections and contributions they were helping us to make in our ongoing exploration of feminist rhetorics. In that way, we were prompted to return to, reconsider, and reframe key concepts, our own analyses, and our engagement with content in the next module with our colleagues' reflections as a deliberate part of that process:

- Consider Judson's guiding questions, "who is speaking and who is being silenced?" and reflection on specific course readings with those questions in mind: "Both essays reclaimed words and texts from those who used it to silence women and brought attention to how vital context, history, culture, and communication frame a world that seeks to control those who challenge it."
- Note Dominique's reminder of the powerful role of critical imagination as a guiding practice in feminist research.
- Regarding rhetorical space and practice, spend time with Kara's post: "My idea of a rhetorical space has been radically improved because before taking this class, I was under the impression that traditional rhetoric was not for women, and that rhetorical spaces were generally those antiquated texts that are continually studied; now, I know that rhetorical spaces exist all around us because texts and speakers are all around us, and rhetoric is for anyone who is willing to think critically about any given rhetorical moment. . . . Before, I did not know that was an option—to generate a new approach to discover solutions to problems that have not been considered (or acknowledged) before."
- Reflect on the questions Dominique poses regarding silences: What silences do these diaries reveal? And recognizing that "One does not need an external audience to perform rhetorical acts . . . how can a writer effectively use silence in rhetoric?"
- Consider, too, how Dominique applies Nedra Reynolds's rhetorical strategy of speaking from—or analyzing from—the margins in multiple ways both in planning for the final project and engaging with readings

and discussion board posts. Note Dominique's reference to a significant keyword connected to our work in feminist rhetorics: counter-narratives. How do/can counter-narratives provide a rhetorical strategy for disrupting dominant narratives and revealing silences?
- See Judson's response to the effect of Royster and Kirsch's geology metaphor as well as feeling of a "tidal wave" in assessing the potential scope of feminist rhetoric. This idea of scope can be both exciting (in terms of possibilities) and overwhelming (in terms of mapping the field). How might we approach our work this semester as an opportunity to find a place for entry or connection in a corner or small section of the work?

Although the structure of online discussion board activities did not always allow for spontaneous discussion and sharing of initial questions as Judson will explore below, these asynchronous discussions also facilitated increased participation from students who might find it difficult to find space to speak up in a face-to-face discussion or synchronous interaction. The nature of the discussion board also allowed for amending or shaping thinking based on engagement with peers' responses and for visible collaborative meaning-making. Finally, as Dominique explained during one of our online writing meetings, the discussion board also allowed for self-rhetoric, "personal rhetorical negotiations that then result in the public presentation of self" (Harrison, 2003, p. 244). Below, both Dominque and Judson illustrate the effects of the internal and external dialogue facilitated by WTL and WTE activities and their effects on facilitating meaningful contributions to communal discourse within and outside of our virtual classroom space.

*Dominique*

My first introduction to feminist rhetoric came not from the prototypical academic readings of feminist researchers, but concrete examples the women in my life displayed, particularly my mother, aunt, and grandmother. At that time, I didn't have the vocabulary to label what I witnessed as feminist actions. These people that the academy noted as unworthy of research, I assumed uninteresting enough to qualify as subjects. How wrong I was. I witnessed how these women moved throughout the world simultaneously handling the patriarchy outside and inside of themselves. And the feminism I witnessed wasn't feminism popularized in early academic feminism because of my family's makeup, which consists of a multicultural Blackness originating from coastal South Carolina, Queens New York, and Jamaica.

My 'proper' introduction, in an academic sense, wasn't through a well-researched, thematically-structured article but a fiction book, *Their Eyes Were Watching God* by Zora Neale Hurston, in my African American literature class—subsequently being by way of the academy. My experience with a single mother and my introduction to Hurston's work sparked an inextinguishable fire, demanding more fuel to feed its roar, pushing me to scour for more Black feminist texts by authors like bell hooks, Joan Morgan, Feminista Jones, and Audre Lorde and the different courses stemming from feminist ideology. This inquiry led me to this feminist-focused rhetoric course. To be clear, I am not your prototypical scholar-in-pursuit. I am not in search of my second or third degree. I am a Black boy from Decatur, Georgia who enjoys grandiose concepts and critical thinking. I was able to work the course into my schedule because of my integrative studies major and with my aspirations of becoming a professional writer, I assumed the class would assist me on my journey.

I'd eventually be proven right repeatedly because of several writing assignments, such as discussion boards and reflections. I was consistently challenged by my peers, my professor, and the material in front of me to think critically about concepts and situations. While the online course format could be seen as a potential dam to free-flowing ideas, I'd argue that it acted more like a tributary, allowing ideas to coast without restraint. Exchanging thoughts through an online medium made it easier to debate difficult topics without fear of retaliation. In-person discussions, while great for fostering immediate and more visceral reactions, do not bode well for someone like myself who has difficulty speaking out loud in a public arena. With the ability to ruminate over my thoughts before presenting them to the discussion board, I participated more willingly and freely. As before when I spoke about witnessing feminism in action without the vocabulary to label it as such, the online assignments allowed me to practice another concept I didn't know the words for, self-rhetoric (Harrison, 2003). With no immediate pressure to respond with an engaging critique, I was allowed to meander on the topic and contemplate my biases to gauge how best to engage with the new idea presented on the discussion board. These WTL activities allowed me to engage critically with theories by way of interrogating the self (McLeod & Maimon, 2000).

Before, I assumed rhetoric was essentially meant to stay in the realm of academia, but after critically engaging with Black women's cookbooks (Collings Eves, 2005) and Southern women's diaries (Harrison, 2003) the mirage was destroyed. Colling Eves's and Harrison's works that surveyed the real-world examples of rhetoric in action gave me something to reference and apply as I viewed spaces I interact with regularly, such as Facebook and Twitter, as locations of rhetoric in action. Now with a new insight into these social media platforms, I regularly find rhetorical value in them. I made a genuine connection with a new concept, I, at first, struggled to comprehend. As a framework, feminist rhetorics, and critical imagination in particular, granted me the thinking tool to critically engage with the concepts, what Palmquist (2020) defines as the goal of WTE activities.

While engaging feminist ideology, I continually encountered voices and perspectives that were excluded in the majority of my studies. I was introduced to the concept of how rhetorical position constructs the ethos of a speaker or writer, how someone's place inside or outside of the margins can affect their perception and how they are perceived, and how voices of the unheard are centered in feminist rhetoric (Reynolds, 1993). Feminist rhetoric reworked my concept of writing from an isolated act of typing onto a white void into a community undertaking. You don't write for yourself or for your papers to die in a hole, but to connect with scholars of the past, present, and future. You write to join the conversation. Which I only understand because of learning about rhetorical position and seeing how the seed of rhetorical study began focusing on communal debates. When we understand writing in general as a communal effort, we start to consider what has been said in the conversation and what we can bring to it.

Before I was introduced to the notion of critical imagination and the ethos of an author through my engagement with the course, I placed my limited perspective on a pedestal, essentially accepting it as truth. First impressions cemented my feelings about particular subjects. There was limited space available for new information to alter my feelings, particularly when it concerned race. Race for me, a disabled Black man somewhat well-versed in the studies of the African Diaspora, is more than theory. It is my life. So much so that, initially, I hated learning about Black history. Too many times, I sat in history class viewing pictures of swaying bodies attached to trees and brutally lashed backs. Those images would often make me queasy, not from the brutality alone, but because those people resembled people on my family tree. Coupled with these experiences was the gratuitous flying of rebel confederate flags I witnessed as a lifetime resident of Georgia. So when, as part of our assigned reading, I had to read Kimberly Harrison's (2003) "Rhetorical Rehearsals: The Construction of Ethos in Confederate Women's Civil War Diaries," I immediately became enraged—partially because of my past experiences with other college courses, specifically regarding history. In one class, I was tasked with arguing for the South's right to disband from the United States, inherently arguing for slavery. Naturally, with this experience in mind, I quickly prejudged the article. What did I, a Black American born and raised in the U.S. South, have to learn from confederate women, the swinging pendulum in the grandfather clock of oppression? Without deviating much from my belief of white women being active participants in oppressing Black people, I read the article. Royster and Kirsch's (2012) critical imagination gave me a blueprint on how to analyze the words before me; I let go of my preconceived notions of truth and knowledge and allowed Harrison, along with the women's diary entries, to tell me their story and location. Without this concept, it would have been impossible for me to consider their struggles. I have even been able to use the concept outside of class and realize that critical imagination is nothing more than an intellectual way of describing empathy. When utilizing critical imagination, we become active participants in the conversation and engage with intent to dissect the information in front of us. I applied the sum of all we learned in the class to my final project: a study of the rhetorical activities of Camille Bell whose son Yusef was murdered during the Atlanta Child Murders. I painted Bell with the fine silk-haired paintbrush of feminist rhetorical knowledge, drawing a detailed depiction of her and her activism. Now I pack this tool with me, tucked into my intellectual painter's pouch, ready for use with all my future projects, spanning from fiction writing to advocacy.

*Judson*

This course was my first experience with feminism and feminist research. I decided to take an American studies course as an elective to fulfill my doctoral coursework and did not know the title of the course until a few days before the semester started. My anxiety was high due to my limited interactions with feminism and feminist thought. Fearing the worst, I quickly memorized that add/drop date for the semester.

However, the first assignment put me at ease. We were tasked with defining and outlining the goal of rhetoric and rhetorical analysis. Bitzer (1968) defines rhetoric by stating that "In short, Rhetoric is a mode of altering reality, not by the direct application of energy to objects, but by the creation of discourse which changes reality through the mediation of thought and action" (p.4). The course used his writings as a starting point for defining rhetoric so that we were able to understand feminism within that frame. I hoped that others in the course would understand that rhetoric was the base alloy of the course and that engaging in such behavior would be key. As we progressed through the curriculum, we would be able to see and engage with each other so that our perspectives would be challenged and further understood. My initial fears of an oppressive course, in which one truth was supreme, quickly dissolved, and I was more willing to listen to what the course, and my classmates, had to say.

Between my experience as a combat veteran and a classroom educator, I felt like I was in a very different place than some of my classmates. This course was also the only one in my program of study that was not designed for educators seeking a graduate degree. Due to the limiting nature of the written word, I was afraid my questioning would be taken as something other than my exploration. In this way, the virtual setting was very challenging. However, I noticed that as the course progressed I was able to maintain an open internal dialogue that helped me try to understand rather than dismiss my classmates' comments and arguments completely. Due to the online format, I had more time which allowed for a slower analysis and, thus, a better understanding of what my classmates and I were trying to say. Our dialogue, both internal and external, allowed knowledge to be co-created just as much as it was individually created. The outside perspectives of my classmates allowed me to see the curriculum in ways that I would have missed in the moment of a physical class. Though limiting, the online format provided space for an internal dialogue that allowed me to engage with perspectives rather than people and thus pushed the boundary of what I accepted as truth. Typically, I have outright dismissed the arguments and thoughts of others while citing my own experience and worldview as proof they were wrong. This time, I was slower to close that door as I sought to understand my perspective while juggling my classmates'.

Throughout the course, I discovered that feminist thought, specifically feminist research methodology, could help serve humanity by providing a critical foundation for analysis and thinking. I took this foundation and asked how I could apply this to my world. As a social studies educator, I sought to create a tool where my students could benefit from the high level of analysis and understanding that I undertook while engaging with the course material. I began to think of feminist research methodology and social studies education as allies. After all, social studies education aims to educate students on how to become citizens capable of critical thinking (National Council for the Social Studies, 2020). I saw feminist research methodologies as a pathway to accomplish this goal.

The flexibility and openness of the final assessment for the course allowed me to explore the literature surrounding feminism, feminist research methodology, and social studies curriculum. Most of the literature focused on the lack of diversity in social studies curriculum and textbooks, which offered minority stereotypes. Some studies called for a feminist research mindset. However, the complete lack of information detailing a feminist research methodology at the middle grades level gave me a blank canvas to start working on a tool that my students could use that blended the goals of both social studies and feminism. Combining both the ideals of citizenship provided by Johnson and Morris (2010) and the categorization of identity provided by Williams (2019), social studies goals aligned with feminist research methodology. Wu's (2010) outline of feminist research methodology bridged the gap between both disciplines and showed that an alliance could indeed be made between social studies education and feminist research methodology. I was also guided by Gurung's (2020) identification and outline of feminist standpoint theory. With this information, I created a tool that could be used in the middle school social studies classroom based on feminist research methodologies.

The CSEW (creation of source, source's message, examination of the source, and the whole picture of the source) was created to allow students to interrogate sources and uncover missing perspectives while helping them reveal systems of oppression. Though it looks like a simple outline or guide, the CSEW form is designed to promote and use critical thinking to determine how sources interact with the world and the systems of domination that stem from such sources. Ideally, students would better understand a historical source through this tool because students would be challenged to analyze a source deeply, "seeing the noticed and the unnoticed, rethinking what is there and not there, and speculating about what could be there instead" (Royster & Kirsch, 2021, p. 20).

This tool aims to disrupt the idea of a perfect source and critically examine it. This examination asks students to look at the creator/author of the source and analyze specific identity markers; analyze and summarize the message; explore the source for both its role in history and the action expected of the audience; and synthesize the whole picture. The final portion of the tool asks students what is missing, what groups might be hurt by the source achieving its goal, and what information is needed to create a complete picture. Allowing students to imagine and seek out other information that might help them understand what's going on is a real goal of feminist research methodology and social studies education. It equips students to understand that the idea that the perfect source exists is flawed, and students should be encouraged to seek out additional information and perspectives. The development and encouragement of such critical imagination and strategic contemplation would help push against the passivity of a traditional social studies course while encouraging students to question sources to better understand them.

This course combined my ideas of what it means to be a patriot and an educator and allowed me to strengthen my resolve to be a better advocate for my students. However, I found that the true lesson of the course was a rediscovery of why I became a teacher. I want to help my students and give them the skillsets necessary to create a more harmonious, pragmatic, and global democratic society. I want them to seek to understand each other and develop a core sense of community and citizenship. This course, especially the development of the final project, allowed me to reengage in these ideas and recommit to them. Ultimately, I was able to bring my passion as a social studies educator to the course and come away with a tool rooted in critical thinking that would help my students develop as competent citizens within their communities.

## Conclusion

As these collective and individual narratives illustrate, feminist rhetorical theories and practices, applied across disciplines, have the potential to shape students' writing and research processes, to support the broader goals of WAC, and to extend the critical thinking of WTE activities. When deliberately guiding course design and WTL activities, feminist rhetorical and pedagogical practices foster collaborative meaning-making and co-construction of knowledge, and they can begin to decenter authority and disrupt hierarchy, centering student voices and amplifying marginalized perspectives. Extending Palmquist's (2020) claims regarding the role of WTE activities "that support students' acquisition and understanding of knowledge central to a discipline, that lead students to work more deeply with that knowledge, and that prepare them to participate in disciplinary discourse" (p. 17), our narratives illustrate how framing these activities within feminist rhetorics allows us to engage in collective meaning-making practices that can reshape that disciplinary knowledge and discourse through a diversity of voices and perspectives. These reflections further demonstrate meaning-making outcomes that were flexible and adaptable for work outside of our course and that demonstrate broader implications for students' roles as change agents. Framed within the affordances of online teaching and learning environments, WTL and WTE activities guided by feminist rhetorical theories and practices facilitate a process of internal and external dialogue that support students' active engagement with and contribution to disciplinary knowledge.

Recognizing "that connection and diversity are keys to sustainability in WAC at this moment in time" (Bartlett, et al., 2020, p.5) and, as Palmquist (2020) reminds us "that designing a successful WTE activity or assignment will involve far more than a deep understanding of critical thinking . . . [and] will require instructors to draw on their expertise as teachers, their experiences as writers, and their awareness of what they must do to provide appropriate feedback to their students" (p. 17), we invite WAC practitioners and scholars to explore the range of possibilities that feminist rhetorical theories and practices may facilitate in achieving these goals. Future work might consider, for example, what WTL activities guided by feminist rhetorics look like in a variety of courses, including those in STEM fields, and how inquiry tools like critical imagination and strategic contemplation may prompt students' engagement with disciplinary knowledge and their advocacy for "seeing the noticed and the unnoticed, rethinking what is there and not there, and speculating about what could be there instead," while "pay[ing] attention to how lived experiences shape our perspectives" (Royster & Kirsch, 2021, p. 20, 22). Recognizing the affordances and possibilities that we address related to online discussions, we also encourage continued explorations of the intersections of feminist rhetorics and WAC in online learning environments, particularly those that further theorize how online discussions may support WTE. Finally, as we have done here, we encourage future work to both theorize and perform "making texts together . . . and forming meaningful collaborations" (Poe, 2020 p. xiii) as an essential part of this process.

# References

Anderson, P., Anson, C.M., Gonyea, R.M., & Paine C. (2015). The contributions of writing to learning and development: Results from a large-scale multi-institutional study. *Research in the Teaching of English*, *50*(2), 199–235.

Bartlett, L. E., Tarabochia, S.L., Olinger, A.R., & Marshall, M.J. (2020). Introduction: On connection, diversity, and resilience in writing across the curriculum. In L. E. Bartlett, S. L. Tarabochia, A. R. Olinger, & M. J. Marshall (Eds.), *Diverse approaches to teaching, learning, and writing across the curriculum: IWAC at 25.* (pp. 3-17). The WAC Clearinghouse/University of Colorado Press.

Berger M. T., & Radeloff, C. (2011). *Transforming scholarship: Why women's and gender studies students are changing themselves and the world*. Routledge.

Bitzer, L. F. (1968). The rhetorical situation. *Philosophy & Rhetoric*, *1*(1), 1–14.

Buchanan, L. & Ryan, K.J. (Eds.) (2010). *Walking and talking feminist rhetorics: Landmark essays and controversies*. Parlor.

Byrne, K. Z. (2000). The roles of campus-based women's centers. *Feminist Teacher*, *13*(1), 48–60.

Chick, N., & Hassell, H. (2009). Don't hate me because I'm virtual": Feminist pedagogy in the online classroom. *Feminist Teacher, 19*(3), 195–215.

Colatrella, C. (2014). Why STEM students need gender studies: Gender studies scholarship and practice contribute to student development and to faculty networking. *Academe, 100*(3).

Collings Eves, R. (2005). Recipe for remembrance: Memory and identity in African-American women's cookbooks. *Rhetoric Review*, *24*(3), 280–297.

Crabtree, R. D., Sapp, D.A., & Licona, A.C. (2009). *Feminist pedagogy: Looking back to move forward*. The Johns Hopkins University Press.

Daniell, B., & Guglielmo, L. (2016). Changing audience, changing ethos. In K. Ryan, N. Myers, & R. Jones. *Rethinking Ethos: A Feminist Ecological Approach to Rhetoric*, SIUP

Ede, L., C. Glenn, and A. Lunsford. (1995). Border crossings: Intersections of rhetoric and feminism. *Rhetorica: A Journal of the History of Rhetoric*, *13*(4), 401–41.

Eodice, M., Geller, E. A., & Lerner, Neal. (2017). What meaningful writing means for students. *Peer Review, 19(*1).

Foss, K. A., Foss, S.K., & Griffin, C.L. (1999). *Feminist rhetorical theories*. Waveland Press, Inc.

Gere, A. R., N. Limlamai, E. Wilson, K. MacDougall Saylor, & R. Pugh. (2019). Writing and conceptual learning in science: An analysis of assignments." *Written Communication*, *36*(1), 99–135.

Guglielmo, L. (2012). Classroom interventions: Feminist pedagogy and interruption. In E. Lay & J. Rich. *Who speaks for writing: Stewardship in writing studies in the 21st Century.* (pp. 102–11). Peter Lang.

Guglielmo, L. (Spring 2009). Feminist online writing courses civic rhetoric, community action, and student success. *Computers and Composition Online,* http://cconlinejournal.org/CCO_Feminism/home.html.

Guglielmo, L. (2019). A right to my language: Personal and professional identity as a 'first generation American-born' teacher-scholar/rhetorician. In L. Guglielmo & S.F. Figueiredo, *Immigrant Scholars in Rhetoric, Composition, and Communication: Memoirs of a First Generation,* NCTE.

Gurung, L. (2020). Feminist standpoint theory: Conceptualization and utility. *Dhaulagiri Journal of Sociology and Anthropology, 14,* 106–15.

Harrison, K. (2003). Rhetorical rehearsals: The construction of ethos in confederate women's civil war diaries. *Rhetoric Review, 22*(3), 243–63.

Imad, M. (2021). Transcending adversity: Trauma-informed educational development. *To Improve the Academy: A Journal of Educational Development, 39*(3), http://dx.doi.org/10.3998/tia.17063888.0039.301.

Johnson, L., & Morris, P. (2010). Towards a framework for critical citizenship education. *Curriculum Journal, 21*(1), 77–96. 10.1080/09585170903560444

McLeod, S. H., & Maimon, E. (2000). Clearing the air: WAC myths and realities. *College English, 62*(5), 573–83.

National Curriculum Standards for Social Studies: Introduction. (2020, January). Social Studies. https://www.socialstudies.org/standards/national-curriculum-standards-social-studies-introduction.

Palmquist, M. (2020). A middle way for WAC: Writing to engage. *The WAC Journal, 31,* 7–22.

Poe, M. (2020). Foreword. In L. E. Bartlett, S. L. Tarabochia, A. R. Olinger, & M. J. Marshall (Eds.), *Diverse approaches to teaching, learning, and writing across the curriculum: IWAC at 25.* (pp. xi-xiv). The WAC Clearinghouse/University of Colorado Press.

Reynolds, N. (1993). *Ethos* as location: New sites for understanding discursive authority. *Rhetoric Review, 11*(2), 325–38.

Reynolds, N. (1998). Interrupting our way to agency: Feminist cultural studies and composition. In S. C. Jarratt & Lynn Worsham (Eds.), *Feminism and composition studies: In other words.* (pp. 58–73). MLA.

Rinehart, J. A. (2002). Collaborative learning, subversive teaching, and activism. In N. A. Naples & K. Bojar (Eds.), *Teaching feminist activism: Strategies from the field* (pp. 22–35) Routledge.

Royster, J. J., Kirsch, G. E., & Bizzell, P. (2012). Feminist rhetorical practices: New horizons for rhetoric, composition, and literacy studies. Southern Illinois University Press.

Ryan, J.D. (2006). Writing the world: The role of advocacy in implementing a feminist pedagogy. *Feminist Teacher, 17*(1), 15–35.

Shrewsbury, C. M. (1987). What is feminist pedagogy? *Women's Studies Quarterly, 15*(3/4), 6–14.

Turpin, C. A. (2007). Feminist praxis, online teaching, and the urban campus. *Feminist Teacher 18*(1), 9–26.

Williams, C. (2019). Developing critical realist comparative methods for researching religions, belief-systems, and education. *Revista Española de Educación Comparada, 33*, 78–105.

# "A long-lasting positive experience" from a Short-term Commitment: The Power of the WAC TA Fellow Role for Disciplinary TAs

ELISABETH L. MILLER AND KATHLEEN DALY WEISSE[1]

> While teaching assistants (TAs) often play a crucial role in teaching writing-intensive courses and often go on into faculty careers, a relatively small body of research has interrogated the ways that WAC/WID programs may effectively train and support disciplinary TAs. In this essay, we draw on surveys and interviews with former WAC TA Fellows—disciplinary TAs who helped to lead training for new TAs teaching writing-intensive courses at a large research university. We offer this close analysis of the WAC TA Fellow role as one relatively short-term and small-scale model with, we find, significant and ongoing benefits for supporting disciplinary TAs as emerging professionals and as future WAC allies.

Teaching assistants (TAs) play a crucial role in university teaching, particularly in introductory and writing-intensive courses. Whether they serve as instructors of record, lead discussion sections, act as graders, or take on other roles, these instructors require training. For writing-intensive courses, this training is often provided by writing across the curriculum and writing in the disciplines programs. Accordingly, these trainings are most commonly (and very competently!) led by writing studies and WAC/WID experts. However, given the philosophy of WAC/WID programs—always drawing on and valuing disciplinary expertise—we analyze in this essay a model of WAC TA training that draws explicitly on the expertise of experienced TAs from across disciplines. Specifically, we examine the WAC TA Fellows role that experienced TAs across disciplines take on to train new TAs teaching an intermediate WID course required for all undergraduate students at University of Wisconsin-Madison, a large public research university in the Upper Midwest. This training, which is held each semester, introduces new TAs to WAC principles that they can use in their upcoming writing-intensive courses and can draw on in their future teaching positions. The WAC TA Fellows are experienced disciplinary TAs

---

1. Elisabeth L. Miller and Kathleen Daly Weisse are co-first authors.

who have been selected by their respective course coordinators to help lead the training based on their own expertise in the classroom and excellence in teaching[2].

As former WAC assistant directors actively engaged in working with TA Fellows—and as WAC and writing program leaders ourselves now—we wanted to learn more about the potential value of this unique way of involving disciplinary TAs in WAC training. Specifically, we wanted to know what former WAC TA Fellows say they took with them from their participation in these roles: for their work as TAs, for their future faculty (or non-academic) careers. What, if anything, stood out about the WAC TA Fellow role to disciplinary TAs? Seeking to add to literature on the need and potential for professional development for graduate student instructors in WAC (Rodrigue, 2013; Cripps et al., 2016) and in academia more broadly (Winter et al., 2018), we sought to explore what TAs across disciplines learn from being put in trainer and leadership roles in a WAC program. Drawing on survey responses and interviews with former WAC TA Fellows, we show the substantial takeaways for disciplinary TAs (and WAC programs) that may come from even a very small-scale role for TAs across disciplines in WAC training. Preparing faculty to be WAC allies, ambassadors (Cripps et al., 2016; Williams & Rodrigue, 2016), or surrogates (Hughes & Miller, 2018), can and—we argue in this essay—*should* begin when they are graduate student TAs. The WAC TA Fellow role offers disciplinary TAs experience taking on WAC leadership in the liminal space of a cross-disciplinary TA training for writing-intensive courses. Such experience is invaluable in the short-term for TAs teaching writing-intensive courses, and in the long-run for TAs who may go on to become faculty ideally positioned to take on powerful WAC pedagogy. We offer this close analysis of the WAC TA Fellow role as one relatively short-term and small-scale model with, we find, significant benefits, for supporting disciplinary TAs as emerging professionals and as future WAC allies.

In what follows, we first provide an overview of the WAC TA Fellow program that we are studying in this essay; we then review literature from WAC and from the scholarship of teaching and learning regarding the needs and options for TA training related to pedagogy—revealing gaps around empirical evidence for the effectiveness of various training models and a growing interest in ways to engage TAs in leadership roles around teaching training. We then lay out our survey and interview-based research designed to contribute to these knowledge gaps. Finally, we analyze those survey and interview responses (which form a rich data set: thirty-three former TAs

---

2. The University of Wisconsin's WAC program officially calls these roles Communications-B (or Comm-B) TA Fellows, as the Fellows support "Communications-B" courses, the intermediate writing-intensive course requirement at the University. To draw on a more universal term for readers beyond the University of Wisconsin, in this article, we refer to these roles as WAC TA Fellows.

hailing from seventeen disciplines across twenty years of this long-standing program) for evidence of what made the WAC TA Fellow role matter to disciplinary TAs.

## The WAC TA Fellow Model

In the WAC TA Fellow model we analyze in this essay, all TAs who are new to teaching intermediate disciplinary writing courses are required to participate in two half-day training sessions that are designed and facilitated by the University of Wisconsin-Madison's writing across the curriculum program. The training is intended to introduce new TAs to key principles of WAC and to equip them with a range of tools and practices they can use in the classroom. Most of the TAs who attend have never taught before. Apart from the required general teaching orientation offered through the graduate program at the university (a training that focuses on general classroom management and HR policies) the WAC TA training (which focuses explicitly on teaching with writing) is the only training that most new TAs receive before entering into the instructor role (with the exception of some individual departments that offer more support).

The WAC TA training is led by the WAC program director, a graduate student assistant director (usually a PhD student in Rhetoric and Writing Studies—a role that the two authors of this essay held previously), and a cohort of experienced WAC TA Fellows (four in the fall semester, to support a training of seventy to seventy-five new TAs, and three in the spring for forty to forty-five new TAs). WAC TA Fellows, who are the centerpiece of our research, are recruited by the WAC program and by writing-intensive course instructors and coordinators, selected based on their success serving as TAs in various disciplinary writing courses. The director and assistant director intentionally recruit fellows, in consultation with course coordinators, from a range of disciplinary backgrounds so as to be representative of the variety of writing-intensive courses offered by the university.

WAC TA Fellows take on a number of tasks during the training. Most notably, they are required to design and facilitate a breakout session centered around a topic of their choosing that is related to teaching with writing. Common breakout session topics include peer review, informal low-stakes writing, and rubric design. TA Fellows also participate in a Q&A panel fielding wide-ranging questions from new TAs, and they lead informal small group discussions during the morning sections of the training—acting as enthusiastic peer models. Fellows draw upon experience teaching writing in their own disciplines when designing materials for the TA training (e.g., running breakout sessions on science writing, effective oral communication, or broader WAC topics such as responding to student writing–supported by examples from their teaching). Oftentimes, this attracts new TAs from similar disciplines who might then prioritize attending their breakout session.

Preparation for the TA Fellow position is highly scaffolded by the WAC program, including a brainstorming session with the WAC assistant director, and a group workshop meeting during which TA Fellows receive feedback on their breakout session materials in an interdisciplinary, collaborative environment. Each breakout session is required to have at least one handout, developed through rigorous peer review by both the WAC staff and the other fellows. Further, each breakout session is designed around principles of active learning and must feature some kind of hands-on or interactive component. Fellows receive a $500 stipend for their work.

Upon completion of the WAC TA training, Fellows attend a debrief session with the WAC program, offering suggestions and feedback on the training, and then receive a thank-you letter featuring positive feedback from training evaluations. These letters are sent out not only to the Fellows themselves, but to their advisors, deans, key stakeholders in departments and colleges, and a selection of other recipients—ranging from former influential teachers to family members—to show appreciation for the hard work they've completed. Altogether, the program is spread across around a month from preparing to training to debriefing.

### Literature Review: Teaching Assistant Training in and beyond WAC

TAs have been the focus of a significant body of scholarship in composition studies, most notably literature about training TAs to teach first-year composition and other general education and core writing courses (Artze-Vega et al., 2013; Macauley et al., 2021). Despite the prevalence of TAs in WAC work, there is scant research on the topic (LaFrance, 2015). Recent calls for more WAC scholarship on TAs, however, seek to change that narrative, pushing researchers to investigate different aspects of the TA experience as they relate to WAC. In their intro to their 2016 special issue of *Across the Disciplines* on TAs and WAC, Williams and Rodrigue, for example, urge researchers to pay closer attention to TAs who, they argue, have the potential to directly and strongly contribute to goals central to the WAC movement. TAs "are worth investing in and supporting," Williams and Rodrigue argue, with the potential to "help us achieve WAC goals in various institutional contexts" (p. 2). In particular, they call on WAC leaders to direct their attention to TAs whose work extends beyond the bounds of the traditional TA role, more specifically, those working with students whose discipline is outside of their own. Elsewhere, Rodrigue (2012) points to gaps in WAC literature around TA professional development. Her 2013 study, which examines how disciplinary TAs perceive themselves as writing instructors and how this perception is influenced by professional development opportunities, serves as a springboard for our research on WAC TA Fellows.

Some scholars have highlighted the unique position of TAs in the academy: noting, in particular, their "liminal" role between student and teacher, between novice and expert (Macauley et al., 2021). That notion has begun to be developed in powerful ways in WAC scholarship. For instance, in her 2016 study, Winzenried, explored how TAs navigate disciplinary genres in the general education classroom by straddling the line between disciplinary "insider" and "boundary crosser." These general education courses, Winzenried argues, offer complex contexts in which TAs "broker" disciplinary genres for students who occupy space on the periphery of disciplines (first- and second-year students who are new to their disciplines or are undeclared). Paying attention to and investing in these TAs' professional development is critical to supporting this challenging and important work. Winzenried stresses that investing in disciplinary TAs' professional development marks a commitment with long-term value, "because TAs often carry the pedagogical strategies and practices they develop in their graduate school teaching experiences into their future faculty positions" (p. 12).

More broadly, the emphasis across academia on supporting graduate students as teachers and as future faculty has intensified over the last couple of decades, particularly as graduate programs have begun to acknowledge that students require training for a range of academic careers, including at comprehensive, regional, or otherwise teaching-intensive institutions (Auten & Twigg, 2015; Winter et al., 2018). One significant effort to address graduate students' need for training in pedagogy is the Preparing Future Faculty (PFF) programming initiated in 1993 by the Council of Graduate Schools and the Association of American Colleges and Universities. PFF programs have sought to address the "recognition that doctoral students aspiring to faculty careers needed preparation for all dimensions of a faculty member's role—teaching, research, service," whereas many existing "models for doctoral education focused on research to the exclusion of other responsibilities" (Winter et al., 2018, p. 3). The PFF initiative funded programming at a wide range of universities, including many programs that continue to thrive and grow (see Rozaitis et al., 2018).

Tracing PFF initiatives and beyond, Kalish et al. (2009) took an inventory of the roughly 290 Carnegie research and doctoral granting institutions in the United States at that time. They found "four types of programming that are much more common than others": teaching orientations, peer mentoring, graduate courses on teaching, and certification programs (Border, 2011; p. xi). A range of scholarship of teaching and learning literature has charted the variety and effectiveness of such programming, particularly arguing for the value of learning communities for future faculty (Richlin & Essington, 2004), and aiming to understand the knowledge and support necessary for graduate students to develop as effective teachers (Austin & McDaniels, 2006).

Our study builds on these important explorations in and beyond WAC scholarship to determine what pedagogical training TAs benefit from. Specifically, we seek to gather empirical insight into the value of one particular teaching development model for disciplinary TAs—joining others' calls for involving graduate student instructors in leadership roles in teacher training and development (Saichaie & Theisen, 2020; Schwaller & Cochran-Miller, 2020; Winter et al., 2018). Rodrigue (2013), for instance, posits that explicit training and education for disciplinary TAs is necessary to enable them to develop identities as writing-intensive instructors. Similarly, LaFrance and Russell (2018) point to the value of providing TAs with hands-on experience with WAC, arguing that "first-hand exposure to WAC research" in an "authentic context" gives graduate students the opportunity to deepen their relationship to writing, learning, and teaching (p. 207). Also closely related to our project, other scholarship has detailed the importance of having disciplinary WAC representatives, acolytes, ambassadors, and surrogates (Hughes & Miller, 2018), but has not focused specifically on disciplinary TAs who serve in WAC leadership positions. The model of WAC leadership around TA training that we examine in this essay has similarities to the WAC Fellowship at CUNY, detailed in Cripps et al.'s 2016 article. While the CUNY WAC Fellowship is an ongoing assistantship, not a short-term, one-time, honorarium-funded opportunity like the WAC TA Fellow role we explore, both fellow roles "help fill the gap" left by a lack of disciplinary pedagogical training. Further, they both provide powerful leadership experiences that build on TAs' liminal roles between student and teacher, as outsiders to disciplines in "preparation for the professoriate" (Cripps et al., 2016). Like the CUNY WAC Fellowship, the WAC TA Fellow role provides an opportunity for experienced TAs to support other teachers by serving as WAC mentors. In our analysis, we seek to further articulate the benefits of the WAC TA Fellow leadership model for TA learning.

## Research Design and Methods

Our IRB-approved survey and interview-based research aimed to answer the following research questions:

1. What, if any, influence has the WAC TA Fellow experience had on former TA Fellows? What have they taken into the rest of their graduate school experiences or into future careers?
2. How do former WAC TA Fellows describe, or characterize, the fellow role?
3. What can WAC practitioners and scholars learn and build on from this training role for disciplinary TAs?

*Data Collection and Analysis*

To answer these research questions, we performed both online surveys and brief (twenty-minute) Zoom interviews. We first obtained a list of 150 former WAC TA Fellows (maintained by the WAC program) who served between the start of the program in 1997 and 2019, for whom we were able to locate ninety-two email addresses. We emailed our ten-question anonymous survey (see Appendix A) via a Qualtrics link to these former fellows. We received thirty-three survey responses, for a thirty-six percent response rate. From those surveys, we gathered ten individuals willing to be interviewed, and we were ultimately able to coordinate eight brief, twenty-minute interviews (two were canceled due to unforeseen life events and conflicts). In interviews, we asked participants to expand on key parts of their survey responses. Table 1 provides a list of the seventeen different graduate programs that survey respondents reported that they were (or are) enrolled in. Table 2 offers a list of interview participants. As Table 2 shows, interviewees served as TA Fellows between 2000 and 2014, coming from eight different disciplines: all now working at universities, and seven of eight still teaching in some capacity.

Using principles of grounded theory (Charmaz, 2014), we collaboratively coded the survey and interview responses, first using open coding looking for the stated values and benefits of the WAC TA Fellows training. Comparing codes, we agreed on two particular categories for analyzing survey and interview responses: a) influences of the WAC TA Fellow role on future faculty (and non-faculty) careers, and b) characteristics of the WAC TA Fellow experience that made it influential.

Table 1

List of Graduate Programs of Former WAC TA Fellow Survey Respondents

| Graduate Program and Number of Participants |
|---|
| Sociology PhD–8 |
| Political Science PhD–3 |
| Theatre Studies PhD–3 |
| Biological Sciences PhD–2 |
| Geography PhD–2 |
| Psychology PhD–2 |
| English -- Literary Studies, PhD–2 |
| Water Resources Management MS–2 |
| English -- Composition & Rhetoric PhD–1 |

| |
|---|
| Communication (Rhetoric, Politics & Culture) PhD–1 |
| Journalism and Mass Communication–1 |
| Scandinavian Studies PhD–1 |
| Human Development and Family Studies PhD–1 |
| History PhD–1 |
| Zoology PhD–1 |
| Life Science Communication (MS)–1 |
| Landscape Architecture MS–1 |
| Total Survey Respondents: 33 |

Table 2
Interview Participants

| Name | Discipline / Degree | Year Served as Fellow | Current Position |
|---|---|---|---|
| Monica | MS Life Sciences Communication | 2000 | Associate Professor of Business Communication |
| Sylvia | PhD Biological Sciences | 2005 | Research Scientist |
| Jacob | PhD Water Resources Management | 2006 | Lab Manager and Adjunct Faculty in Biology |
| Sam | PhD Theatre Research | 2007 | Associate Professor of Theatre |
| Manasi | PhD Journalism & Mass Communication | 2009 | Professor of Journalism and Mass Communication |
| Susan | PhD Interdisciplinary Theatre Studies | 2011 | Lecturer in Theatre Studies and Accountant in the Medical School |
| Kyle | PhD English – Literary Studies | 2012 | Assistant Professor in a Continuing Studies program |
| Abbey | PhD Communication (Rhetoric, Politics, Culture) | 2014 | Associate Professor in Communication (Rhetoric, Politics and Culture) |

## Analyzing WAC TA Fellows' Experiences

In these analysis sections, we draw from survey responses as well as some more in-depth examples from interviews with past TA Fellows to explore two key questions: "What were the influences of the training on WAC TA Fellows?" And, subsequently, "What characteristics of the TA Fellow role made it influential for Fellows?" For the first question, four significant themes arose: TA Fellows frequently mentioned developing a newfound appreciation for teaching writing and talking about teaching writing. Second, many participants discussed appreciation for having the opportunity to build community with other like-minded teachers across disciplines. Third, a number of respondents said their experience prepared them to take on future teacher trainer roles. Finally, a large majority of the TA Fellows said they continue to return to the WAC materials they had designed. Following this analysis of what mattered to TA Fellows, we then turn to a discussion about what exactly made the training so meaningful—particularly its link to funding, recognition, individualized attention, and leadership. It is worth noting that there is an interesting slippage between WAC TA Fellows' discussions of powerful teaching and teaching training and the impact and import of teaching with writing or training others to teach with writing. We find that slippage to, in fact, provide noteworthy evidence for just how central teaching with writing and foundational WAC pedagogy is to powerful teaching writ large.

*Tracing Influences of the WAC TA Fellow Role on Disciplinary TAs*

*Refining teaching knowledge.* Despite the brevity of the TA Fellow experience (the entire process typically takes no longer than a month from the time that the fellow accepts the position to the conclusion of the training), it had a significant impact for those involved. "I consider it one of the more rewarding and memorable teaching experiences during my graduate career," said a 2013 fellow completing a MS in water resources management. TA Fellow Monica even went so far as to claim, "I feel comfortable saying that it influenced my, like, entire career." These findings are akin to what Cripps et al. (2016) noted from their own fellows study: that the fellowship opportunity gave TA Fellows an opportunity to critically reflect on WAC pedagogy, and that pedagogical experience, in turn, "helped them feel like better teachers in their disciplines" by the time the fellowship was concluded (p. 6).

In our analysis, we found that many survey respondents/interviewees attributed the enthusiasm they feel for teaching directly to their experience as WAC TA Fellows. In this way, their responses point to the program's reach and impact. Importantly, for some of these participants, well over a decade had passed since they had served as WAC TA Fellows, yet the experience remained fresh in their minds. For some participants, this memory stood out as their sole experience with formal pedagogical training. As one former TA Fellow from sociology who graduated in 2013 said, "There really weren't other opportunities like this when I was in grad school." For others, it was one of the only times they could connect with others about teaching. In her interview, Abbey, a communications PhD who served as a fellow in 2014, expressed regret that she hadn't had the opportunity to work with TAs in other disciplines earlier in her graduate career, explaining, "Because teaching isn't valued at an R1 in other disciplines, you kind of have to talk on the [down low] in, like, these kind of hidden underground networks to be like 'Hey, what do you know?' and I just remember feeling like I was really cobbling these [networks] together…so the idea that there were other people [fellows] who could also design workshops and who are also thinking about teaching and interested in doing it well, and happy to talk about it, like, all of that was super valuable and kind of mind-blowing." Likewise, former TA Fellow Jacob noted in his interview that there was a significant gap filled by the WAC TA Fellow experience, saying "nobody was really looking after us in terms of you know where our careers were going if we were getting teaching experience" until the WAC TA training.

In addition to these rare and powerful opportunities to focus on teaching, many of our study participants noted that being asked to help *train* TAs in other disciplines helped them develop more confidence in their teaching, resulting in a mindset shift about the purpose of TAships in general. A former fellow from sociology who is now an associate professor recalled that the experience "definitely focused positive attention on the role of a teaching assistant," which "often isn't seen as a position of value in the academy." Along those same lines, in his interview, Kyle, a literary studies PhD and now an assistant professor, explained, "I think that one thing I learned is just how important (and sometimes rare) it is to have conversations around writing pedagogy with college instructors—from TAs to professors." The WAC TA Fellow model treats TAs as future faculty whose pedagogical development is equally as important as that of more senior faculty across campus.

Others expressed specific appreciation for the unique opportunity to work with TAs outside of their individual disciplines. A fellow from 2003 who received their PhD in sociology and now works as the director of service learning at a major research university explained in their survey response, "[T]he TA Fellow was such an amazing opportunity to dig deep into the specifics of how we teach, and at the same time, do that with people from all different disciplines. To explore what writing means in different contexts, and how to make that explicit and teach it, rather than leave it implicit. It gives you a perspective that there are so many ways to do things, and we academics are so wedded to our own silos sometimes, that we don't even remember that folks in different departments see writing very differently than we do." Sam, a TA Fellow completing a PhD in theatre, and now an associate professor, shared this appreciation for the ways being exposed to other disciplines and their writing and communication conventions helped to hone teaching knowledge and practice. He now teaches first-year seminars with students across disciplines and explained the value of being able to make connections across a range of majors. The WAC TA Fellow experience helped reveal nuances across disciplines, putting what may have been taken for granted practices into context and making visible the ways in which these practices have been shaped to fit different pedagogical and disciplinary needs across the curriculum. For TAs who occupy liminal roles in the classroom, serving as both insider and boundary crosser to their discipline (Winzenried), finding these connections among one another helped them to untangle some of the complexities of writing-intensive instruction and to even more deeply develop and refine their teaching expertise.

*Building a teaching community.* In addition to expanding teaching knowledge, the ability to work with TAs across disciplines invoked in some participants a deep appreciation for building community around teaching. Susan, a 2016 fellow who was at the time pursuing her PhD in theatre said, "I suppose the thing that has stuck with me most was how pleasurable it was to be in a community of folks who were passionate about teaching writing—especially across disciplines." As a first-generation college student, Susan had struggled against feelings of "imposter syndrome" and "a little bit like I'm just trying to catch up to my peers." The WAC TA Fellow experience was a "refreshing and exciting" opportunity to connect with others and share goals/insights about teaching with writing. Another survey response from a 2010 fellow from sociology explained, "I learned how important communities of practice are to becoming an effective teacher of writing. Joining with colleagues from across the university helped me recognize our common challenges and rewards." Serving as a WAC TA Fellow offered participants a language for articulating the shared values they felt around teaching. As one survey participant remarked, the TA Fellow position "continued to strengthen my understanding of teaching as a process. I learned a ton from the other fellows." These findings resonate with and provide additional texture to Rodrigue's (2013) conclusion that WAC training deepens disciplinary TA's teaching identities.

The WAC TA Fellow experience even inspired others to seek out similar communities of practice later in their faculty careers. For some cohorts of fellows, these relationships extended beyond the boundaries of the WAC TA training experience. Whether through casual friendship or through joint membership in a writing group, these connections demonstrate, as one participant argued, that "the program fostered long-lasting relationships among alumni" in different disciplines. Susan's cohort of TA Fellows, for instance, went on to develop "a long-standing relationship" by forming a joint writing group following the conclusion of their WAC TA Fellow duties.

"I felt a little bit like I was finding my people," she explained. "At a huge research institution that, like, intimidated me...I felt like I had a hard time finding my people, and this was one location where it was like, oh this feels kind of custom made to find, you know, like-minded folks." Bringing together these small cohorts of TAs enabled these productive communities to form. The fact that they formed around WAC is no-doubt a boon to the field as these TAs continued on to become future faculty at a number of high-profile institutions across the country.

This WAC teaching community provided a place to push back on less rhetorically grounded views of teaching. WAC practitioners have historically fought against models of writing education that privilege grammar and mechanics as the sole markers of writerly success (Russell, 2002). Likewise, the TAs in our study found that the WAC TA Fellow role helped them, like Susan mentioned, to find powerful spaces of belonging, to counter imposter syndrome, and even to push back against what they now see as an unproductive and harmful pedagogical approach. Thinking back to her time as a TA Fellow, Abbey explained, "Because of the experience...I could set aside some of the more toxic teaching practices I saw modeled in other places." Sam, a 2007 fellow studying theatre research, echoed these sentiments, claiming that his time as a TA fellow "made me a passionate defender of students, and made me dislike instructors who constantly complained about their terrible students."

*Transitioning from teacher to teacher-trainer, student to faculty.* Several survey respondents, including a sociology PhD, mentioned that their involvement with TA Fellows "was some of the only leadership/training experiences I had as a graduate student." The WAC TA Fellow role engaged graduate students not only in being trained, but in the powerful leadership role of trainer. In this way, the WAC TA Fellow role provides the kind of TA leadership experience that many Preparing Future Faculty (PFF) initiatives strive for (See Saichaie & Theisen, 2020; Schwaller & Cochran-Miller, 2020; Winter et al., 2018). A theatre and drama PhD, now a teaching professor and an academic advisor, explained that they "first discovered [their] love for teaching teachers and mentoring TAs." Discovering that passion gave them a sense of "confidence" knowing they had the "skills to be able to help" others "become better pedagogues." They described their "work as a fellow" having long-lasting effects: "find[ing] its way into" their classroom instruction, presenting at "national conferences about teaching theatre and mentoring TAs," serving in professional organizations on the topic of teaching, receiving teaching awards and recognition, and "running two pilot programs for student success and retention."

Similarly, a sociology PhD TA Fellow in 2003 reported that they "now work in faculty development for community engagement," and they consider their experience as a TA Fellow to be "one of the reasons for my success as a faculty member, and the opportunities I've had to benefit from—and now work in—faculty development."

What's more, the exposure to WAC/WID philosophies and their "variation across the university" as a TA Fellow "has proved very useful," they say, in their current faculty development role: particularly preparing them "for the range of attitudes faculty members have towards faculty development and pedagogical training, which is not always positive! All of these insights I use regularly in my current position." Similarly, acknowledging how training and leadership roles are often a part of faculty careers, a composition studies TA Fellow, now an associate professor, reflected that "It's just good to learn how to train other new teachers," noting that they now "regularly" train new composition instructors.

Former TA Fellows also appreciated the trainer role for the way it extended their "influence." "Being a trainer allowed me to influence many more TAs, to improve the writing experience for students," said a sociology PhD who served as a fellow in 2014 and now is a management and program analyst for the administration for Native Americans. A MS in water resources management who was a TA Fellow in 2013, and now a postdoc, described their enthusiasm and increased investment as a trainer: "I learned that I enjoyed the trainer role, and I found myself wishing for [more] opportunities to engage with writing as a teacher/trainer." "As a trainer," they explained, "I was more enthusiastic about the material than I was as a participant; I was invested in the outcome of the training in a different way than I was as a participant." We take these reflections on the power of experiencing the trainer role to be evidence of the kind of "fly-on-the-wall view of pedagogy in action, without being a direct participant as either a student or instructor" that Cripps et al. (2016, p. 2) identify as an especially impactful benefit of engaging disciplinary TAs in WAC work.

This different, or increased, level of investment as a trainer appeared in the responses of several other participants. A survey respondent who served as a TA Fellow from the MA program in landscape architecture described the value of being "asked to evaluate my teaching approaches or strategies and identify a concrete example that I could share." This kind of "active assessment" of their teaching was a new and challenging task that deepened and strengthened their knowledge of their own teaching practices. Similarly, our interviewees Susan and Manasi provided insights into the value of serving as a trainer. "I think as a trainer I actually learned more than when I was new," reflected Susan, a TA Fellow from theatre studies. That deepened learning, Susan went on, came from the fact that she "felt like an insider (part of the community), and because I was focused less on contributing something worthwhile and instead really listened to all of the great ideas/experiences my fellow TAs had. Also simply preparing for the training really upped my learning game." Manasi concurred, observing that, though she already had significant teaching experience prior to enrolling in her doctoral program in journalism, she was motivated by supporting the "many other TAs" who "were totally new to teaching." Mentoring new TAs and "[o]rganizing events with meticulous planning" were both valuable takeaways from Manasi's participation in the trainer role of TA Fellow.

Other respondents described their fellow roles as, one human development and family studies PhD student said, supporting them in "learn[ing] how to transition from student to leader and to be a student educator." The power of this kind of leadership experience was especially apparent for one of our interviewees, Kyle, now an assistant professor and director of a community education program who described his TA Fellow experience helping him to "reflect and kind of think about why and what kinds of things I was hoping to accomplish and what worked and what didn't"—a kind of "self-awareness" he took from the experience. Kyle's reflection on developing leadership skills he took to his faculty career clearly resonates with calls to involve graduate students in the "leadership and administrative" elements of programs designed to prepare future faculty (Winter et al., 2020, p. 5).

What's more, Kyle reflected on the TA Fellow role being "pivotal" in his "shifting from" student to professor. Citing the fact that graduate students often experience imposter syndrome, Kyle explained how serving as a TA Fellow helped him "go from somebody who wants to do something to somebody who knows that they can do something." Reflecting on his own teaching practices and "sharing them with other teachers," and ultimately "see[ing] they were helpful" gave Kyle a deep sense of confidence that "maybe I have something to actually offer, versus just somebody who's trying to figure out what to do." In a final interview comment, Kyle expanded on the value of this self-awareness, self-assurance, and sense of purpose: "It was just the first time that I was offered a position where I did feel as though I could take what I had learned and spread it in a way that would have a ripple effect: that it was beyond just the students in my classroom" and might "actually affect the classrooms that I'll never know, that I'll never be a part of, but that those TAs would go out and create, and I love that idea." This "ripple effect," Kyle said, "was a pivotal thing for me as a grad student" being able to envision a faculty career. Such a "ripple effect" begins by centering deep WAC experience in a TA's pedagogical and administrative philosophy, which spread outward and forward into their faculty careers. This, we believe, is just the kind of truly powerful payoff that can come from a WAC program's investment in TAs (a finding that lends more credence to Williams and Rodrigue's urging for WAC programs to prioritize disciplinary TAs [2016]).

*Creating and using materials and resources.* Many participants said that they continue to refer back to and actively use the materials and resources they both received and designed for the WAC TA training. A 2003 fellow and now a professor of political science at a small liberal arts college continues to use these materials almost twenty years later: "I have a folder in my office called 'teaching writing' and all that material is still in there, at my fingertips, to use. It's been incredibly helpful across the years."

In fact, continuing to use resources from the training, including the handouts created for the fellows' individual breakout sessions, years later in their careers was the most prevalent trend we found in survey and interview responses.

Still, many others remarked on the value of this program for their CV. A 2013 fellow from sociology and now an associate professor of sociology, remarked, "It was really good leadership practice in the realm of teaching. There really weren't other opportunities like this when I was in grad school. I think it looked good on my CV also, which was useful for the job market." Similarly, Jacob, a former biology WAC TA Fellow, found his materials helpful when going on the job market the semester following his time as a TA Fellow. A 2012 political science TA Fellow said that the TA training was critical to their success on the job market, sharing that they "had tangible experiences I could point to during job interviews where I had taught writing!" For many fellows, it was the direct and authentic experience training teachers and talking about teaching writing that mattered most.

## Unpacking the Characteristics that Made the WAC TA Fellow Role Valuable for Fellows

In the previous section, we discussed what influences the WAC TA Fellow role has on graduate students as they serve as TAs and as they go into faculty and non-academic careers. In this section, we explore the characteristics of the fellow role that allow for, or enable, these effects. Particularly given that the WAC TA Fellow role is a relatively small one, and quite a long time ago for many of our respondents, what makes this experience compelling to fellows, and what makes it valuable? What makes it stick, or what makes it, as Sylvia, a PhD from biological sciences who served as a fellow in 2005, calls "a long-lasting positive experience"? We discuss here how funding, recognition, and program leadership make this role so successful.

The $500 stipend for the WAC TA Fellow role incentivized this position for several TAs. One history PhD graduating in 2021 described being "interested to learn from other TA Fellows to improve" their own teaching and to "pass along some of the things I had learned," but they emphasized that the "$500 also helped me justify setting aside the time this role required." Likewise, one sociology TA Fellow noted that "the money was a great incentive." Sylvia considered the funding and the benefits she accrued from the fellow experience as more than fair for the work required. "I guess I just look back at that experience, even though it was just a couple of days, and I think I got maybe $500 for it, it was just, you know, it wasn't much, but the value for it, the cost benefit kind of value is actually pretty high," Sylvia reasoned.

Appreciation for the recognition and honor of the WAC TA Fellow role also appeared in former fellows' responses. That recognition happens at multiple levels. Jacob, a TA for an honors biology course, explained that he agreed to serve as a TA

Fellow primarily due to his deep respect for the course coordinators from that program, who asked him to serve as a fellow. A sense of honor and recognition also stemmed from TA Fellows' sense that their experience and expertise were being valued. "I was honored to take on the leadership role because I grew so much as a teacher as a WAC TA and found the experience to be such a rewarding one," described a Scandinavian studies PhD, now an associate professor and department chair. Sylvia similarly described a sense that, by "being selected as a WAC TA Fellow," that her "input was valued and that I had something worthwhile to share with other student TAs. It was an honor to participate."

While memories of the funding or recognition WAC TA Fellows provided were "hazy" for some, many still vividly recalled the WAC program's leadership. One, now associate professor in political science, clearly remembered the WAC director's "energy, enthusiasm, and support of TAs!" A former fellow and MA in landscape architecture echoed these sentiments, expressing their "respect" for the director and their "excitement and dedication to writing as an art and educational tool that should be accessible to everyone." Sam, likewise, spoke of the WAC facilitators—including the director and the graduate student assistant director—as "great leaders," "mentors," and "sounding boards."

This enthusiastic, supportive leadership manifested, for many former TA Fellows, in what Abbey explained as the "individual attention" provided by WAC facilitators—a very productive "back and forth conversation" about faculty development that she has taken on to her faculty career. "I recall receiving helpful, individualized formative feedback" from WAC facilitators as they prepared their training materials, said a 2010 TA Fellow from psychology, now a professor. "I remember feeling surprised by the level of attention given to my plan, and a consequent sense of confidence that my presentation would be helpful for those who attended my session," they added.

Citing the preparatory meetings with other fellows and WAC facilitators, the MA in landscape architecture expressed their appreciation for WAC facilitators making them "feel welcomed, appreciated" and "set[ting] an environment where I felt quite connected to the other WAC TA Fellows." They attributed this ethos directly to the enthusiasm and personal approach of the WAC director: "I think if [the director's] approach had been more impersonal, the personal connection, support, and encouragement I felt for my other WAC TA Fellows (and that I believe was reciprocated) would not have occurred and would have led to less exciting and dedicated presentations." Finally, a 2013 TA Fellow and current postdoc in water resources management described the power of "one-on-one engagement" provided to prepare the fellows to lead training sessions. They commented on a "specific meeting" to discuss training session plans with the WAC TA assistant director, receiving 'thoughtful" feedback, and "feeling like [the assistant director] valued my ideas for the lesson." This "collaborative" meeting made them feel "excited about the Fellow role."

## Concluding Thoughts and Takeaways

The argument could be made that a program like WAC TA Fellows is a "boutique" kind of model. That is, while the WAC TA training at the University of Wisconsin-Madison is attended by roughly 110–120 graduate TAs each year, the WAC TA Fellows role is held by just seven TAs per year—no more than five percent or so of the TAs involved in our training. In a university with roughly 10,000 graduate students at any given time, this number may feel staggeringly small. So, then, what makes this model worthwhile? For one, involving and training TAs to be leaders in WAC training helps grow our numbers of WAC acolytes, ambassadors, and surrogates; once the TA Fellow experience is over, these graduate students return to their home discipline equipped with new WAC knowledge to impart to their colleagues. These effects are, indeed, long-lasting—a finding that shows up in the vivid descriptions of former WAC TA Fellows, some of whom participated in the program roughly twenty years ago.

In addition to being long-lasting, the position is far-reaching, extending out to a significantly larger network of people beyond just those who held the position. This TA Fellow model, as our research has shown, has helped spur the development of multiple sustainable teaching communities over the years—at the University of Wisconsin-Madison and beyond. By emphasizing shared values and a shared enthusiasm for teaching among TA Fellows during the workshopping process, the program was able to foster these strong, ongoing professional relationships. Similar to our participants, we, as WAC assistant directors, found that having these types of relationships in graduate school was extremely valuable for supporting our efforts in the classroom, on the job market, and in our future careers. Notably, though, these were opportunities that would have been very difficult to find on our own, outside of the WAC TA Fellow experience and our engagement with it. The pre-training workshopping stage of WAC TA Fellow training specifically helped model a teaching community environment where participants could share openly about the challenges they face in their writing and teaching—an ethos that TA Fellows brought into the WAC TA training as well. Finally, recruiting and training TA Fellows offers WAC practitioners a way to contribute to preparing future faculty, particularly when there may be few other options available. The exceptional TAs who are recommended for the WAC TA Fellow position have already shown an interest in teaching and are likely to go on to become faculty with teaching responsibilities following their graduate career. For some of these TA Fellows, however, the WAC TA Fellow role was the only training they received on teaching. By involving disciplinary TAs in leadership roles, WAC practitioners can thus provide much needed, impactful support for those who might have otherwise gone without any explicit pedagogical training.

One of the TA Fellows we interviewed, Monica, was particularly enthusiastic about the potential for this program to be taken up elsewhere, noting, "I would love for it to be modeled at other universities." We share this belief in the efficacy and value of this particular model for developing and supporting disciplinary TAs in, and through, WAC work. As explored in our second analysis section, the TA Fellow role was influential for a number of reasons: specifically, it provided funding, recognition, individualized attention, and supportive leadership. While other programs that take up this model do not have to mirror ours, we believe that some mix of these four key characteristics should remain constant for ensuring TA support. It's the combination of these four characteristics that make our program successful. Without funding, WAC TA Fellows lack incentive. Without recognition, the perceived value of the program for one's career diminishes. Without individualized attention, the WAC principles that we rely on TA Fellows to know may fall to the wayside. And without supportive leadership, the program becomes less sustainable, and the burden of labor placed on the WAC TA Fellows starts to outweigh the benefits of participating.

We could imagine the WAC TA Fellow model being used to train graduate TAs for leading or co-leading one-time or ongoing WAC faculty workshops or WAC consultations. As our research has shown, for a range of TAs with such diverse disciplinary backgrounds, even short-term leadership roles may have significant long-term impacts. Through a WAC TA Fellow model, WAC programs can tap into the powerful talents of experienced disciplinary TAs (following Williams and Rodrigue's 2016 call). With powerful benefits in terms of building teaching communities, filling gaps in teacher training for future faculty, and fostering positive disciplinary perspectives on writing, this WAC TA Fellow role can positively contribute to disciplinary TAs' development as teachers, teacher trainers, and professionals, while promoting foundational WAC pedagogy.

## Acknowledgments

The authors wish to thank the study participants for sharing their time and experience, the two anonymous reviewers for their formative feedback, *WAC Journal* editors for their guidance and support, and Brad Hughes for his unflaggingly generous mentorship and powerful leadership.

## References

Artze-Vega, I., Bowdon, M., Emmons, K., Eodice, M., Hess, S., Lamonica, C., & Nelms, G. (2013). Privileging Pedagogy: Composition, Rhetoric, and Faculty Development. *College Composition and Communication*, 65(1), 162–184.

Austin, A. and McDaniels, M. (2006). "Preparing the professoriate of the future: Graduate student socialization for faculty roles." Higher Education: Handbook of Theory and Research, edited by John Smart, pp. 397–456. Springer.

Auten, J. and Twigg, M. (2015). "Teaching and learning SoTL: Preparing future faculty in a pedagogy course." *Teaching & Learning Inquiry.* 3(1). pp. 3–13.

Border, L. B., ed. (2011). Mapping the Range of Graduate Student Professional Development. *Studies in Graduate and Professional Development.* New Forums Press.

Charmaz, K. (2014). Constructing grounded theory (2nd ed.). SAGE Publications.

Cripps, M. J., Hall, J., & Robinson, H. M. (2016). "A way to talk about the institution as opposed to just my field": WAC fellowships and graduate student professional development. *Across the Disciplines. 13*(3).

Hughes, B. and Miller, E.L. (2018). WAC seminar participants as surrogate WAC consultants: Disciplinary faculty developing and deploying WAC expertise. *The WAC Journal,* 29, 7-41. https://wac.colostate.edu/docs/journal/vol29/hughes_miller.pdf

Kalish, A.S., Robinson, S., Border, L., Chandler, E., Connolly, M., Eaton, L.J, Gilmore, J. (2011). "Steps toward a framework for an intended curriculum for graduate and professional students: How we talk about what we do." In *Mapping the Range of Graduate Student Professional Development, Studies in Graduate and Professional Development,* edited by L. B. Border, New Forums Press, pp. 163–173.

LaFrance, M. (2015). Making visible labor issues in writing across the curriculum: A call for research. *College Composition and Communication, 67*(1), A13–A16.

LaFrance, M. and Russell, A. (2018). "Preparing Writing Studies graduate students within authentic WAC-Contexts: A research methods course and WAC program review crossover project as a critical site of situated learning." *The WAC Journal,* 29, pp. 207–229.

Macauley, W., Anglesey, A. Edwards, B., Lambrecht, K., and Lovas, P., Eds. (2021). *Standing at the Threshold: Working through Liminality in the Composition and Rhetoric TAship.* University Press of Colorado.

Richlin L. and Essington, A. (2004). "Faculty learning communities for preparing future faculty." *New Directions for Teaching and Learning,* 97, pp. 149–157.

Rodrigue, T. K. (2012). The (in)visible world of teaching assistants in the disciplines: Preparing TAs to teach writing. *Across the Disciplines,* 9(1). https://wac.colostate.edu/docs/atd/articles/rodrigue2012.pdf

Rodrigue, T. K. (2013). Listening across the curriculum: What disciplinary TAs can teach us about TA professional development in the teaching of writing. *Teaching/Writing: The Journal of Writing Teacher Education, 2*(2). https://scholarworks.wmich.edu/wte/vol2/iss2/5/

Rozaitis, B., Baepler, P., Gonzalez, A., Ching, P, Wingert, D., & Alexander, I.D. (2020). "Preparing future faculty: Pedagogical practice in graduate School." New Directions for Teaching and Learning, no. 163. pp. 35–43.

Russell, D. (2002). *Writing in the Academic Disciplines, 1870-1990: A Curricular History*. 2nd ed. Carbondale: Southern Illinois UP.

Saichaie, K. and Theisen C. H. (2020). "Editors' notes." *New Directions for Teaching and Learning*, no. 163. pp. 7–12.

Schwaller, E.J. and Miller-Cochran, S. (2020). "Writing pedagogy education: Preparing and professionalizing graduate students as writing instructors." *New Directions for Teaching and Learning*, no. 163. pp. 65–72.

Williams, A. & Rodrigue, T. (2016, September 30). TAs and the teaching of writing across the curriculum: Introduction. *Across the Disciplines*, 13(3).

Winter, K., Kent, J., & Bradshaw, R. (2018). Preparing future faculty: A framework for design and evaluation at the university level. Council of Graduate Schools.

Winzenried, M. A. (2016, September 30). Brokering disciplinary writing: TAs and the teaching of writing across the disciplines. *Across the Disciplines*, 13(3).

## Appendix A

*Survey*

Thank you very much for completing this survey about your experiences as a WAC TA Fellow (helping to lead the WAC TA training at _____ alongside _____ and the Writing Across the Curriculum program).

This IRB-approved study seeks to learn more about the potential effects and value of this opportunity for Teaching Assistants (TAs) across disciplines.

The survey below should only take about 15 minutes or so to answer. Your answers will be entirely anonymous. The last question on the survey asks if you would be willing to participate in an entirely optional follow-up interview (just 20 minutes), expanding on your survey responses. If you choose "yes," you'll be contacted via the email you provide.

Feel free to reach out to the researcher, _____.

Thank you again for your time and participation!
1. What year did you graduate (or do you expect to graduate) from _____?
2. What program are/were you enrolled in?
3. What is your current occupation (or most recent or significant post-graduate employment)?

4. Have you done any teaching with writing since acting as a WAC TA Fellow? If so, what kinds of teaching?
5. If you recall, could you explain why you decided to take on the WAC TA Fellow leadership role?
6. Describe one or two vivid memories of your time as a WAC TA Fellow at _____ (preparing for the event with _____ & the WAC program, leading a breakout session in the training for new TAs, participating in the Q&A panel with other WAC TA fellows, facilitating informal discussion groups with new TAs).
7. What, if anything, do you think you learned from being in the trainer role as a WAC TA Fellow, versus the participant/new TA role?
8. How did the role of WAC TA Fellow fit into, or compare to, other training / teaching / leadership experiences you had as a graduate student?
9. How, if at all, do you think your experience as a WAC TA Fellow has contributed to, or informed, any of your subsequent work (teaching, administrative or leadership work, etc.)?
10. Are there any other comments you wish to make about the WAC TA Fellow role or your experience with it?
11. OPTIONAL: Would you be willing to participate in a roughly 20-minute interview via Zoom about your experiences as a WAC TA Fellow?

*Interview*

# Conversations in Process: Two Dynamic Program Builders Talk about Adapting WAC for Trilingual Hong Kong

## TERRY MYERS ZAWACKI

One need only look at recent writing studies publications—those published in the International Exchanges on the Study of Writing series, for example—to chart WAC's increasing interest in transnational approaches to teaching writing in and across the disciplines, particularly in regions where English is an additional language and scholars often draw on different theoretical traditions. And the interest is mutual, as evidenced by the growing number of international scholars and practitioners attending IWAC conferences over the past many years, including the two dynamic and dedicated English Across the Curriculum (EAC) program builders introduced here—Julia Chen from the Hong Kong Polytechnic University (PolyU) and Jose Lai from The Chinese University of Hong Kong (CUHK). Julia's and Jose's work may already be familiar to many of you who may have attended their panels at IWAC conferences, which is where I first met Julia in 2014. Shortly after that, Julia visited a number of notable US WAC programs to inform the fledgling EAC initiative, including George Mason's where I had directed the program until retiring. A year later, in 2015, EAC was launched in Hong Kong with an international conference for which Jose was one of the organizers and I one of the plenary speakers. Since that time, I've had the privilege of working with both Julia and Jose on a number of their innovative EAC projects. For this interview, I've asked them to talk about why and how the EAC initiative was developed, including the changes in the structure of higher education that provided the exigence, the influence of WAC on its design, current EAC projects, and the cross-institutional collaborations that have contributed to its sustainability.

But let me begin with a brief description of the EAC initiative, a WAC-adaptation that focuses on both writing and speaking in English. At the outset, EAC, which grew out of a 2013 cross-disciplinary community of practice at PolyU, was supported through a government inter-university learning and teaching fund. To win this funding, in 2014 Julia invited three universities—CUHK, the Hong Kong University of Science and Technology, and City University of Hong Kong—to join

PolyU in bidding for a grant through the University Grants Committee (UGC), an independent professional advisor to the Hong Kong government on the funding and development of the higher education sector. The funded project—*Professional Development in English Across the Curriculum (EAC)*—was first presented at a symposium for English teachers from local universities, with planning already underway for an international conference to be held the following year to introduce this new initiative far and wide.

Led by a cross-institutional team, EAC, like WAC, has been guided by the key premise that programs and practices are always best developed locally, responsive to differing institutional contexts and exigencies. Also like WAC, the collaborating EAC institutions share a central goal of extending the teaching of English writing and speaking to faculties (colleges), departments, programs and courses across the curriculum. To accomplish this goal, the English language teaching units have taken the lead, variously establishing communities of practice (CoPs) with instructors in other disciplines, creating discipline-focused writing and speaking courses or workshops and materials, and developing innovative approaches like the mobile app Julia and colleagues designed and the peer tutoring initiative Jose launched, both of which they describe here.

And now I've talked enough, so with that preamble, I'll turn the conversation over to Julia and Jose, starting with a question about the trilingual context of Hong Kong, which necessitates making significant adaptations to any WAC-like program that's adopted.

**Terry Zawacki**: I'm a little embarrassed to admit, Julia, that until I attended your 2014 IWAC session about your efforts to create a writing and speaking across the curriculum initiative, I knew very little about language use in Hong Kong, other than that both English and Cantonese are used, and even less about educational policies around languages used in the schools, particularly after the Handover to China. Let's start there.

**Julia Chen**: With the 1997 Handover, Hong Kong was returned from British rule to Chinese rule, and the following year the government introduced a new "Medium of Instruction" policy wherein three-fourths of previously English-medium secondary schools switched to Chinese-medium teaching. In contrast, the vast majority of universities in Hong Kong use English as the medium of instruction, and all assessments, apart from those related to other languages, are to be completed in English, which is difficult for many students who only had to write up to 300 words in English in secondary school.

The current language education policy says its aim is that students will become biliterate and trilingual with the expectation that secondary school graduates will be proficient in writing Chinese and English and able to communicate in Cantonese, English, and Putonghua. While this is the policy, many students in Hong Kong universities, such as in my university with its research and teaching mission, enter with a rather low English proficiency level. [Note: Putonghua, or standard Mandarin, is the language used in schools and workplaces in mainland China. Chinese refers to the written form with traditional and/or simplified characters.]

**Jose Lai**: CUHK, a comprehensive research university established in 1963, is the only university in Hong Kong that adopts a bilingual language policy whereby both English and Chinese are considered official languages on campus. Depending on the nature of the programs, faculties are free to choose their medium of instruction and students are free to choose whichever language they want to operate in unless it is specified by the faculty. For example, within the same course, students may hand in their written assignments either in English or in Chinese. Since English is used as a second or foreign language, it is not difficult to understand that students have a strong preference for Chinese, their native language. So it has been our real challenge to help the university achieve their goal of making their graduates "globally competitive" and able to use English as an international language. With students' relatively low motivation in using English, perhaps it's not too exaggerating to say that we have to fight an uphill battle trying to enhance students' English language proficiency in general and academic literacy in specific.

**JC**: On a 2016 government survey of students and economically active professionals, respondents rated their Cantonese competence at around 87 percent, so much higher than the 25–29 percent ratings they gave for their spoken and written English. At the same time, they rated the frequency of using written English at work considerably higher than that for spoken English or Cantonese, which tells us that we should focus our EAC efforts on students' writing abilities since there seems to be so much more for them to learn about writing than about speaking, the different academic/disciplinary genres of writing, for example.

**TZ**: I know that there were changes in the structure of higher education after the Handover, so will you each explain what those were and how the changes led to the adaptations in the writing and speaking curricula and also motivated the EAC scheme?

**JL**: It was not so much about the Handover but the proposed territory-wide education reform which covers the curricula, the assessment mechanisms, as well as the admission systems for different stages of education. More importantly, it involved the implementation of a new normative *four-year* undergraduate program, known as the 3+3+4 program to replace the former *three-year* undergraduate program (seven years of secondary and three years of tertiary education). This means freshmen will have received one less year of advanced English training at the secondary level prior to entering a university. To facilitate the implementation of this new education system, in 2008, the University Grants Committee, the funding agent of all government funded universities, organized symposia to encourage exchanges among all institutions. The biggest impact of this change in the education system that took effect in 2012 was the perceived need of English language enhancement for the freshmen, so having a first-year foundation English program was considered crucial. At CUHK, the English Language Teaching Unit (ELTU) was naturally entrusted with the task of designing a new English curriculum that now spans over three years to meet the students' academic literacy needs.

**JC:** In a number of universities in Hong Kong, but not including Jose's bilingual university, almost all subjects are done in English except for Chinese subjects. Moving from a three-year to a four-year undergraduate curriculum, however, has not necessarily meant more curriculum space for standalone English proficiency courses offered by the English language center. This means that students often have no English courses in many of the following semesters in their four-year undergraduate curriculum. At the same time, feedback from academic faculty and English language teachers indicates that students often exhibit a lack of transfer of the generic academic English skills they learnt in these compulsory courses. In my university, many of our undergraduate degree students enter with a bare pass in the post-secondary public English exam, and, while their English at university exit is a little better, employers' feedback says our graduates are weak at English. That is why my colleague Dr. Grace Lim and I saw the need to start EAC to offer more English learning support to students.

**TZ:** I'm curious why you chose WAC as a model for EAC rather than CLIL, which would likely be more familiar to many education professionals in Hong Kong, especially at the secondary level, given the British/European influence.

**JC:** Content and Language Integrated Learning, CLIL, aims to help students learn both the content and the language appropriate to that content in the same subject; for example, a CLIL geography course puts equal focus and time on teaching students climatic characteristics in different regions and the English used to describe those climatic characteristics. But CLIL typically requires a re-write of the whole course to provide that equal focus on content and language. Plus, finding suitable teachers who can teach the content and also have language teaching qualifications is a challenge, especially in places like Hong Kong where content teachers are generally non-native speakers of English who do not have confidence to teach English. Finding curriculum space to teach the remaining fifty percent of the content that has been taken out of a CLIL course is not easy either. So it was more feasible to introduce some language elements in an existing content course without disrupting the flow of the course and without taking up a lot of class time on language learning. And we also decided to have language teachers work with subject teachers to offer course-related English resources that they can use with their students or give out to students, e.g., a lab report for engineering courses with a lab component. So this is why WAC was chosen.

JL: I'll add that I don't believe we can talk about WAC as a model for EAC without mentioning an earlier WAC initiative that dates back to 2004 when my former colleague, Dr George Braine, started WAC in Hong Kong at CUHK and brought it over to two other universities, PolyU and City University. Call it serendipity, call it fate, it is interesting to note that after a decade WAC was rekindled in the form of EAC at PolyU with CUHK joining the project in 2014. To develop the project at CUHK, I was joined by another colleague, Dr Damian Fitzpatrick, to reach out to both administrators and academic staff. As Director of the English Language Teaching Unit, I started talking to department and program chairs about our vision, while Dr Fitzpatrick talked to individual faculty members he came into contact with. Interestingly, the first early adopter from the School of Architecture was recruited by Damian from the athletic field. Another early adopter was our Pro-Vice-Chancellor Professor Isabella Poon from the Statistics Department. She believed that it would be strategic of her as PVC to join the project to testify to its worth and practicality before we reached out to the significant others. The following year, she offered the ELTU extra funding to conduct a one-year EAC communities of practice pilot project, which in turn laid the foundation for that project to be fully funded from 2016 to the present. I speculate that part of the reason why PVC Poon would place such good faith in our EAC movement is because she had experienced WAC back in 2004 and found the practice impressive. She once lamented over the fact that the WAC project had to be discontinued at the time due to the ending of funding. So right from the outset, I've been very conscious of its sustainability, and our team has worked doubly hard to making it a regular practice within our university.

TZ: Speaking of sustainability, I'm wondering about the current status of the cross-institutional movement. Has there been any new grant funding for EAC initiatives? And, Julia, what about internal PolyU support for EAC efforts there? How is EAC going to be sustained, in other words?

JC: In 2017 the HK government again called for learning and teaching project proposals that involve multiple universities, but the project focus had to be different from the last round. Since mobile use was becoming more popular, I suggested to the other universities that we apply for this new fund to develop a mobile app to offer discipline-related English language tips to help students write their capstone projects. The app includes an assignments calendar, a chat function to talk with professors, plus specific support for assigned projects. Unfortunately, the cross-university mobile app project funding ran out in August 2021, but I have found some funding from my own university for the app, which four universities continue to use. During these years, I've also encouraged academic staff (faculty) and English language teachers in my university to apply for funding to do EAC in their own courses, and I am glad that there have been at least six funded EAC projects led by PolyU academic staff (i.e., not English teachers) and at least one by English language teachers. I'm trying to sustain EAC as much as I can at PolyU and the other collaborating universities. Besides the small grants I received to continue the Ninja mobile app, as we named it, I've also received a cross-institution grant to create an AI-assisted virtual platform to help students with academic presentations. I co-lead this project with a PolyU engineering faculty member. Hong Kong Baptist University will collaborate with us. I'm always looking for new funding sources, which requires ongoing program assessment. Our textual analysis of student writing, some with pre- and post-EAC intervention and some just post-EAC, for example, showed a heightened sense of awareness of key writing features brought up in our EAC discipline-specific support materials.

**JL**: At CUHK, we see EAC as a complementary component of the ELTU credit-bearing core curriculum. While ELTU can provide formal faculty-based language course training within a particular discipline, EAC allows us to flexibly cater to the needs of program-based or even course-based settings by offering different forms of intervention, including communities of practice, thereby encouraging faculty to take greater ownership of language education. With EAC we also aim to cultivate a culture of non-academic/creative writing on campus (e.g., reflective writing, memoir, poetry, and short stories through various means, such as organizing workshops and competitions), and we are incorporating eLearning components, such as the mobile app, micro-modules, and eLearning platforms. The assessment data we have—survey data with students and learning outcomes as reported by our department or academic program collaborators—all point to the encouraging findings that the EAC interventions have been successful. New collaborators have also been recommended to us by word of mouth. Some collaborators are even willing to provide funding and/or manpower support should our funding run out in the future. They, too, care about the sustainability of EAC, which they treasure.

**TZ:** You've both talked about some of your EAC successes, but are there additional successes you'd like to mention? And what about disappointments?

**JL:** Along with the successes I've already mentioned, I guess it would be the increasing number of collaborations with content teachers over the years and the retention of nearly all early adopters with high satisfaction levels on surveys we administer. Another indicator would be the expressed hope from the senior management to make EAC a flagship program of the university and their plan to provide recurrent funding for its implementation. I also expect that the scope of work for EAC will expand to include close collaboration with the university General Education Program with some corresponding funding forthcoming. If I have to list any disappointment, it would be the cessation of some cross-faculty collaborations due to circumstances such as the movement of participating content teachers or a course no longer on offer.

**JC:** I'll start with disappointments, which involves the rejection of a sustainability proposal I wrote that included EAC successes I'll mention shortly. Even though the proposal was supported by the Learning and Teaching Committee, it was rejected in September 2016 by the university senate and its chair, the university president, who did not see the need to institutionalize EAC. As a result, there is no regular university funding for EAC, so we have to keep looking for project funding elsewhere. But to focus on successes—perhaps my biggest success has been resuscitating WAC in Hong Kong after previous attempts were discontinued and getting four other universities on board the EAC project. Internally, at least twenty out of the twenty-nine departments in PolyU have participated in EAC and, as I've mentioned, we have academic and ELTU teachers spreading the fire by applying for EAC funding. And even though my sustainability proposal was rejected, we have an EAC that includes many academics from the disciplines. Since 2013 we have had an EAC community of practice, and we continue to offer staff development seminars and other forms of support to students. And I have plans to try to get the new university management to keep funding EAC every triennium, although my plan does not include another paper to the Senate.

**TZ:** Now, as we continue to talk about successes, Jose, will you describe your Peer Tutoring Scheme (PTS), a project inspired by the launching of EAC at CUHK? How did you decide to embark on this initiative?

**JL:** I am always passionate about service-learning, which involves students learning through training, experience and reflection. With this zeal, I started to brainstorm the possibility of introducing peer tutoring in speaking and writing as service-learning as early as the new 3+3+4 curriculum was implemented in 2012. Peer tutoring was also in line with the non-formal "soft approach" to language enhancement the ELTU was proposing to complement the formal curriculum. With the launching of EAC, which is operative at the program/course level, I thought it appropriate that a personal level of support be given to students, particularly for those who tend to shy away from formal learning settings. I wanted to recruit peer tutors from across the curriculum into this service-learning opportunity to share their experience and knowledge of speaking and writing in general and within the disciplines.

Since peer tutoring is a service rather than a paid job, our tutors are only expected to serve at least an hour (i.e., one session) but they can meet up to seventeen hours per week as stipulated by the university. Tutees cannot exceed four one-hour sessions per week. We are indeed fortunate to have an average of some fifty peer tutors per year, and they come from all eight faculties and around fifteen countries/regions. This diverse profile has inarguably contributed to the attraction and success of PTS. Based on this success, we're hopeful that funding will be continued, and PTS will be here to stay especially when one of our university's new initiatives is service learning, as stated in the university's recent strategic plan.

**TZ:** Julia, to the list of successes you've already mentioned, I'd also add the English Across the Curriculum conference volume you published in the International Exchanges series on the WAC Clearinghouse, and, of course, the three international EAC conferences you've organized and hosted at PolyU. Would you talk a bit about these accomplishments?

**JC:** The first EAC conference came about when we realized we had no WAC experts in HK who could give advice or share WAC experiences and insights. We decided to create a focused opportunity, a conference, to be held over two to three intensive days, for participants to learn about WAC, and also CLIL, from experts and presenters elsewhere. We also wanted to spread the word that we are starting EAC in HK, and we wanted to establish a profile for our EAC work to get senior management buy-in.

Four universities—those I've already mentioned—comprised the organizing committee for the first conference. We wanted big names for plenary speakers to draw participants, so we invited Terry Myers Zawacki, whom I'd met in the US, and Ursula Wingate, a CLIL scholar from the UK who had spent time in Hong Kong. For the third plenary, we purposefully chose a chemistry professor from the University of Missouri, whom I'd also met in the US. The first conference in 2015 was held at PolyU with 240 registrants. The second conference in 2018 was organized only by PolyU and again we invited big names from WAC, CLIL, and TESOL as plenaries, including Mike Palmquist for WAC. This conference drew registrants from twenty-two regions and countries, which brings me to the 2021 virtual conference, which was organized by a five-university team. This time we had over 1,000 registrants from forty-eight regions and countries and 200 presenters! As before, plenaries included CLIL scholars and a WAC panel with Terry, Mike, and Marty Townsend that replaced invited speaker Michelle Cox [now Michelle Crow] who had to withdraw for health reasons.

An outcome of the second, 2018, EAC conference was the volume *English Across the Curriculum: Voices from around the World*, edited by a PolyU team and published in 2021 in the International Exchanges series, as Terry mentioned, with hard copies available from the University Press of Colorado. Our goal in this peer-reviewed collection was to show how EAC, WAC, and CLIL are developing around the world based on the range of presentations at the conference. (https://wac.colostate.edu/books/international/eac2018/).

**TZ**: Finally, in the midst of all of this professional activity, will you tell readers a little about yourselves? Your backgrounds? Your avocations?

**JC**: I was born in Hong Kong, but I did high school and my undergraduate degree in physics and astronomy in Canada, as well as my masters in TESOL and PhD in applied linguistics. I'm currently the director of the Educational Development Centre at PolyU and associate professor (courtesy) in the Department of English. Music is my pastime. I play the piano and lead a worship team for my church. I have a fellowship in singing performance from Trinity College London (FTCL) and have performed in operas and concerts as a soprano soloist. In 2014 I gave a solo concert at the Hong Kong City Hall Concert Hall to raise funds for homeless children, which raised over a million Hong Kong dollars with over 1,000 people attending. When I retire from university, I will likely take up some singing teaching.

**JL**: I spent my formative years in Australia attending senior high school and receiving all tertiary education there, including a BA and MA at the University of Sydney in English and linguistics and my PhD at Macquarie University in applied linguistics. Currently, I'm director of the English Language Teaching Unit, which is staffed by some sixty language educators and more than ten administrative and project support staff. I lead the unit in curriculum design, review, and development. In my spare time, if any, I enjoy sports, music, and planting in pots. Above all, I treasure spending time with family and friends, and in particular, my two grandbabies.

**TZ**: Thank you both so much for the time you spent answering my many questions, only some of which I've been able to include here. For now, I'm crossing my fingers that there will be a fourth EAC international conference when everyone will be able to meet in person once again.

*Flashback Articles*

# They

## AMY WARENDA

> If a woman is swept off a ship into the water, the cry is 'Man overboard!' If she is killed by a hit-and-run driver, the charge is 'manslaughter.' If she is injured on the job, the coverage is 'workman's compensation.' But if she arrives at a threshold marked 'Men Only,' she knows the admonition is not intended to bar animals or plants or inanimate objects. It is meant for her.
>
> —Alma Graham

> "I corrected a boy for writing 'no one..they' instead of 'no one...he,' explaining that 'no one' was singular. But he said, 'How do you know it was a he?'"
>
> —A teacher (Miller 38)

Observers have long pointed out the ambiguity of the use of the pronoun *HE* in generic contexts and the advantages of having a true generic singular pronoun, which would be sex-neutral.[1] In the absence of such a sex neutral pronoun, speakers of English have been expected to utter sentences such as "Everybody should bring his book tomorrow," where the "everybody" referred to includes forty women and just one man. For centuries, speakers and writers of English have been happily getting around this obstacle by using *THEY* in such situations, yielding sentences such as "Everybody should bring their book tomorrow." Unfortunately, since the middle of the eighteenth century, prescriptive grammarians have been prescribing the use of *HE* in these situations and attacking the use of *THEY*, by arguing that the use of *THEY* is a violation of the rule for pronoun agreement, that is, a singular noun such as "everybody" should not take a plural pronoun such as *THEY* (Frank 72).

Although the prescriptive grammarians have not explained why it is all right for a female person such as "Mary" to be referred to by a masculine pronoun such as *HE*, they have managed to make many people feel guilty about breaking the law when they use *THEY* in such sentences (Frank 73). This is not the way it should

---

1. This article first appeared in *WAC Journal*, Volume 4, April 1993.

be. Because the English language lacks an acceptable singular non-gender-specific pronoun, the singular use of *THEY* to fill this void should be deemed acceptable.

## Is 'He' She'?

The first grammars of modern English were written in the sixteenth and seventeenth centuries at a time when formal schooling was only offered to boys. The male authors of these earliest English grammars wrote for male readers in an age when few women were literate. It is the belief of both Casey Miller and this author that the masculine-gender pronouns grammarians used in grammatical examples and generalizations did not reflect a belief that masculine pronouns could refer to both sexes.

They reflected the reality of male cultural dominance and the male-centered world view that resulted. Males were perceived as the standard representatives of the human species, females as something else (Miller 35–36). This was clearly exhibited by the way women were treated as property.

Present-day linguists, tracing the history of the socalled generic *HE*, have found that it was invented and prescribed by the grammarians themselves in an attempt to change long-established English usage. The object of the grammarians' intervention was the widespread acceptance of *THEY* as a singular pronoun, as in Lord Chesterfield's remark (1759), "If a person is born of a gloomy temper...they cannot help it." Nearly three centuries earlier, England's first printer, William Caxton, had written, "Each of them should . . . make themselfready," and the invocation "God send everyone their heart's desire" is from Shakespeare. In such usages, grammarians argued, *THEY* lacked the important syntactical feature of agreement in number with a singular antecedent. But in prescribing *HE* as the alternative, they dismissed as unimportant a lack of agreement in gender with a feminine antecedent (Miller 36).

In 1850, the British Parliament passed an actual law concerning the use of *HE* as a generic pronoun. In an attempt to shorten the language in its legislation, the Parliament declared: "in all acts, words importing the masculine gender shall be deemed and taken to include females" (Frank 73). In simpler days it was certainly acceptable to refer to a genderless noun such as "customer" with masculine pronouns. But *HE* never has and never will call to mind the picture of a woman (Seifert 34).

When a adult sees a hawk riding a thermal updraft and says to a child, "Look at him soar!" the child not only learns something about how hawks fly but also that all hawks are male and, by implication, that maleness is the norm (Miller 44).

As a linguistic device imposed on the language rather than a natural development arising from a broad consensus, "generic" *HE* is fatally flawed. This fact has been demonstrated in several recent systematic investigations of how people of both sexes use and understand personal pronouns. The studies confirm that in spoken usage, from the speech of young children to the conversation of university professors, *HE* is rarely intended or understood to include *SHE*. On the contrary, at all levels of education people whose native tongue is English seem to know that *HE, HIM,* and *HIS* are gender-specific and cannot do the double duty asked of them (Miller 38). *HE* brings a male image to mind, and it does so whether editors, authors, nomads or acrobats are the subject (Miller 38). Yet use of the pronouns *HE, HIS,* and *HIM* to refer to any unspecified or hypothetical person who may either be female or male is usually justified on two grounds. First, the practice is said to be an ancient rule of English grammar long and faithfully followed by educated speakers and writers. Second, it is asserted, somewhat paradoxically, that the usage is thought to distinguish the educated from the uneducated—that everybody knows *HE* includes *SHE* in generalizations. Historical and psychological research in the past few years have produced evidence to refute both claims (Miller 35).

Feminist scholars maintain that the generic *HE* and similar words "not only reflect a history of male domination" but also "actively encourage its perpetuation." For example, the ostensibly generic use of *HE* has permitted varying legal interpretations that often exclude women but always include men (Gastil 630). In 1879, for example, a move to admit female physicians to the all-male Massachusetts Medical Society was effectively blocked on the grounds that the society's by-laws describing membership used the pronoun *HE* (Miller 37). It seems that even the "educated" individuals are having a difficult time trying to find a standard rule for *HE*. More and more writers and speakers seem to agree with the feeling expressed by psychologist Wendy Martyna, who wrote, *HE* deserves to live out its days doing what it has always done best—referring to 'he' and not 'she'" (Miller 38).

## What's in a Pronoun?

Rather than rely on authority or opinion, some scholars have conducted experiments to determine whether or not today's speakers of English perceive the forms *MAN* and *HE* as generic. In one study, Joseph Schneider and Sally Hacker asked some students to find appropriate illustrations for an anthropology book with chapter headings like "Man And His Environment," and "Man And His Family"; another group of students was given titles like "Family Life" and "Urban Life." The students who were assigned titles with the word *Man* chose more illustrations of men only, while the second group chose more pictures showing men, women and children. Other studies have confirmed the tendency to interpret *HE* and *MAN* as masculine unless the context clearly indicates they are meant generically, the contrary of what is usually claimed. One experiment conducted by Wendy Martyna that tested the usage and meaning of these words among young people, found that women and men may be using the terms quite differently. The men's usage appears to be based on sex-specific (male) imagery while the women's usage is based instead on the prescription that *HE* should be used when the sex of the person is not specified (Frank 73-74).

Studies conducted by Janet Shilbley Hyde, a professor of psychology at the University of Wisconsin, suggest that when people read or hear *HE*, they do not think neuter. They think male. One of Hyde's experiments tested 132 third and fifth graders who were asked to rate how well women and men could do each of several jobs: teacher; doctor; fireman or firefighter (half of the subjects were asked about the former the other half about the latter); and a fourth occupation, "wudgemaker," which was fictitious and presumably gender-neutral. Wudgemaker, of course, was her target. Hyde's results showed that the children formed strong perceptions about a person's ability to make wudges depending on the pronoun that was used in describing what a wudgemaker does. Women were rated as least able to do the job when the description used *HE;* they were rated most able to do the job when *SHE* was used in describing the duties. When neutral words or phrases were used in the description ( *THEY,* and *HE* or *SHE),* men and women were both seen as able to do the job. Said Hyde: "It can be concluded that the use of *HE* affects the stereotyping of occupations, or the schema of an occupation that children form. When children hear *HE,* even in an explicitly gender-neutral sentence, they are overwhelmingly likely to think of a male" (Borgeois 41).

Many investigators have found the male bias of the generic *HE* to be very common among high school and college students (Gastil 230). The impression that has been derived from the writings of older college students has been that many, perhaps most, of those adults use singular *THEY* as their pronoun of choice (Meyers 229). I conducted my own study to confirm this notion and found that it was indeed true. I asked my First-year Composition class to choose between three sentences, one with *HE,* one with *SHE* and one with *THEY,* which one they would most likely use in their writing. The class unanimously chose "Everyone should be sure to bring *THEIR* book to class tomorrow" to refer to a group containing both males and females. The professor opted to decline all three choices and instead make up one of his own: "All should be sure to bring their books tomorrow." This is an example of a common way writers and speakers deal with the lack of a true non-gender-specific pronoun; they avoid entirely the use of sentences that require such pronouns (Frank 72-73).

## He, She And Thon?

Among the many gender-related reforms proposed for the English language, the creation of a common-gender pronoun to replace the generic masculine *HE* in a sentence like "Everyone loves his mother" stands out as the one most often advocated and attempted and the one that has most often failed (Baron 190). There have been a series of proposals with the aim of eliminating the "pseudo-generic" use of the pronoun *HE*. Some advocate the introduction of a new sex-neutral third person singular pronoun such as *THON* to replace *HE* in situations where either sex may be meant, as in "A doctor should be careful that thon (he) does not misdiagnose." Others advocate the use of *HE* or *SHE*, or recasting the sentence in the plural as in "Doctors should be careful that they do not misdiagnose" (Frank 84). In all, more than eighty bisexual pronouns, little words such as *NE, TER, HEER, ET* and *IP* have been proposed since the eighteenth century (Baron 190). None has found overwhelming favor with the public, however, and all have therefore been pushed aside and forgotten.

A number of books have appeared using *SHE* in generic situation, and some writers have compromised with *SHE* or *HE*. The trouble with *HE* or *SHE* form is that it becomes awkward when repeated (Miller 41). *S/HE* is a nice orthographic trick, but it is unusable either in the spoken language or in other grammatical cases: *HER/HIM* and *HER/HIS* do not collapse so neatly (Frank 87). There has also been some support for the extension of *IT* in place of the generic masculine. *A Woman's New World Dictionary* (1973) defines *IT* as a "third person neuter pronoun now acceptable to use when sex of the referent is not known. Examples: The baby was happy with its rattle; the applicant signed its name." Critics of *IT* point to its impersonal nature as their main argument against its adoption (Baron 192).

Another proposal to eliminate the generic use of *HE* is by recognizing the legitimacy of using *THEY* or *THEIR* (Frank 84). Unfortunately, the singular use of *THEY* is still deemed unacceptable for written usage. As might be expected, this solution is widely used in spoken English, even by "educated" speakers (Seifert 35). Some grammarians approve of the singular *THEY.* For example, Alexander Bain, in *A Higher English Grammar* (1879) defends its use: "When both genders are implied, it is allowable to use the plural...Grammarians frequently call this construction an error: not reflecting that it is equally an error to apply 'his' to feminine subjects. The best writers furnish examples of the use of the plural as a mode of getting out of the difficulty" (Baron 193). In the syntax volume of his *Grammar* (1931), George Curme accepts the literary evidence of singular *THEY,* but he wrongly concludes that it is an obsolescent construction which survives only in "loose colloquial and popular speech." In *A Grammar of Contemporary English* (1972), Randolph Quirk and his coauthors set forth a more tolerant version of this position. Singular *THEY* is labeled the informal construction, and generic *HE* the formal unmarked one, while coordinate *HE* or *SHE* is rejected as "cumbersome" (Baron 193-194).

## They: Only Logical

Singular *THEY* has a long history in Modern English, stretching back to the mid-sixteenth century, and a distinguished one—it occurs in the works of Addison, Austen, Fielding, Chesterfield, Ruskin, and Scott, to cite only a few major English writers, and the *Oxford English Dictionary* notes that the absence of a singular common-gender pronoun renders "this violation of grammatical concord sometimes necessary" (Baron 193). Singular *THEY* is widely used in speech and writing and, despite the stigma of ungrammaticality that has become attached to it since the eighteenth century, the construction shows no signs of dying out. The occurrence of the plural pronoun *THEY* in reference to indefinite nouns such as *PERSON, SOMEONE* or *EVERYONE,* which are singular in form but often plural in meaning, is another example of semantic concord in English overriding grammatical concord (Baron 192-193). When we need a non-gender-specific pronoun in speech we say *THEY.* If we speak English that way today, knowing that the usage is "incorrect," we will probably be writing it that way soon. Grammar, after all, both prescribes how we "ought" to use the language and how we *do* use it (Seifert 35).

Once upon a time *YOU* was a plural pronoun only.

It assumed its singular function in the days before prescriptive grammarians were around to inhibit that kind of change. English needs a comparable third person singular pronoun, and for many *THEY* meets the need (Miller 39). Singular *THEY* has held its own against the grammarians and the antifeminists, and there are some writers who remain optimistic that singular *THEY* will one day become acceptable (Baron 196).

The case of sex-indefinite *THEY* versus generic *HE* is a special and complex one. The contest has been long and controversial, and teachers and prescriptivists have invested a great deal of energy in the fight for the "correctness" of *HE*. They have succeeded in modifying our formal written English and in creating a collective guilty conscience among speakers of English with even a few years of schooling. But they have not managed to uproot *THEY* from colloquial usage, and today, some groups of feminists have unburdened themselves of their guilty conscience and are openly advocating this usage. They know that "Everybody must pay *their* taxes" is, unfortunately, more accurate than "Everybody must pay *his* taxes" (Frank 87).

*Flashback Article*

# Translation, Transformation, and "Taking it Back": Moving between Face-to-Face and Online Writing in the Disciplines

HEIDI SKURAT HARRIS, TAWNYA LUBBES,
NANCY KNOWLES, AND JACOB HARRIS

Faculty teaching face-to-face (F2F) may dread transitioning to online instruction.[1] While scholars have addressed this trepidation for writing faculty (see Warnock; Hewett and Ehmann), this hesitancy can be compounded for faculty across the disciplines who seek to transform both content and writing assignments from the physical to the digital classroom. Online course management systems (CMS) can hinder this task because these systems employ teacher-centered rather than participatory models (Palmquist 406). In addition, developing online courses requires that faculty modify their current pedagogy, often while continuing to juggle their face-to-face courses. Even for seasoned faculty, preparing and delivering an online course can be time-consuming, taking three times as long as a F2F course (Palloff and Pratt 74). In "Online Teaching and Classroom Change: The Trans-classroom Teacher in the Age of the Internet," Susan Lowes calls teachers who are transitioning from F2F to online instruction "trans-classroom teachers," likening them to immigrants "leav[ing] the familiarity of the face-to-face classroom for the uncharted terrain of the online environment, whose constraints and affordances often lead to very different practices." The immigrant metaphor is apt, as instructors transitioning to digital culture must adapt to new problems, behaviors, languages, attitudes, and identities.

Before coming together for a faculty professional development workshop in Summer 2011, each of the authors—faculty members at Eastern Oregon University from English and Writing, Education, and Religious Studies—had faced the challenges of "immigration" alone in our separate disciplines. As we shared our processes of moving our F2F courses online, we found ourselves describing three distinct stages. First, we attempted to "translate" successful F2F strategies into the online environment. In this translation stage, we replicated the F2F activities, assessments, and assignments with little thought about the effect on pedagogy of the change in modality. After initial failed attempts at direct translation, we "transformed" our practice, adjusting

---

1. This article first appeared in *WAC Journal*, Volume 25, Fall 2014.

our pedagogy to make it more applicable for online delivery. When the CCCC released the 2013 "Position Statement of Principles and Example Effective Practices for Online Writing Instruction (OWI)," we discovered that practices we had arrived at organically through trial and error, alone in our disciplines, were reflected in the experiences of expert online writing instructors across the country.

Even more importantly, perhaps, our conversations about online instruction surfaced a third stage in our pedagogical processes: based on online student success, we found ourselves modifying our F2F practices, "taking back" to the F2F classroom improved activities, scaffolding, and feedback. Thus, transformation of online writing instruction does not represent the conclusion of a neat, linear progression. Instead, regardless of discipline, online delivery can become an integral component of recursive pedagogical practice, in essence, acting as a distancing strategy for thinking through F2F content delivery.

## Online Writing Across the Curriculum

Enrollment in online courses has grown steadily in the past ten years. The Babson Group indicates that 32% of college students are enrolled in at least one online course, and online courses were a "critical component" of the long-term strategy at 69% of all higher education institutions in the U.S. (Allen and Seaman 4). However, the implementation of online writing classes often precedes substantive research into sound online writing instruction practices, particularly writing across the curriculum (WAC) online. Research into writing instruction in fully-online classrooms has primarily focused on composition or writing studies classrooms (see the CCCC OWI Bibliography).[1]

Research into WAC work in regard to computer-mediated instruction focuses most often on F2F, networked classrooms or hybrid courses. Donna Reiss, Dickie Self, and Art Young's collection *Electronic Communication Across the Curriculum* (1998) includes guides to implementing computer-mediated instruction across the curriculum, but the only chapter in the book dedicated to online education describes a course that works primarily through email in an era before Facebook, YouTube, or the rise of Google (Chadwick and Dorbolo). More recent work addressing online WAC has focused on assessing online writing (Dean), and even that work has focused on hybrid rather than fully-online courses. A special edition of *Across the Disciplines* titled "Writing Technologies and Writing Across the Curriculum" presumes that online resources and websites primarily serve on-campus or hybrid classes. The most recent survey of WAC programs (2010) gives only brief mention to "electronic technologies" in WAC programs. Chris Thaiss and Tara Porter write, "we can state that the great majority of our respondents did not see the growth of electronic technology per se closely connected to their idea of WAC" (557). In this survey research, "technology" is equated with the implementation of course-management systems and other digital tools in the service of F2F learning. Perhaps the most complete collection to date regarding online WAC is Neff and Whithaus' *Writing Across Distances and Disciplines,* which acknowledges "many writing and writing-intensive courses delivered from a distance have not reached their potential" (2). In spite of increasing numbers of students taking online classes and higher education's emphasis on increasing online programs, the literature in WAC has not substantially focused on the affordances and constraints of online writing instruction across the curriculum.

While research in computer-mediated or networked classrooms can inform online instruction, effective online classrooms face one challenge not found in either computer-mediated or hybrid classrooms. As Ken Gilliam and Shannon Wooten state:

> The best parts of composition pedagogy are precisely what's missing in most online learning situations. Indeed, the very characteristics of online learning that make it most attractive in university recruitment campaigns—the convenience of learning outside of real time, the ability to work from home or on the go—are the very things that disembody learners, separating them physically and temporally from their professors and classmates. (para. 4)

Online separation from a classroom and disciplinary community may impede the writing process, as students struggle to hone the purpose of their writing with a disembodied audience, to trust their disembodied peers and instructor with authentic communication, and to provide and implement feedback that occurs only in writing, without connection to the spoken words, laughter, and body language that might provide additional guidance and support.

In 2007, the Conference on College Composition and Communication Executive Committee responded to the need for research addressing the teaching of writing in fully online environments by charging the Committee for Best Practices in Online Writing Instruction to develop a position statement, which became the "Position Statement of Principles and Example Effective Practices for Online Writing Instruction" (CCCC OWI; CCCC "Establishing") and represents a starting point for further research into online WAC.

The CCCC OWI Position Statement acknowledges the need for online instruction not only to "translate" but also to "transform" instructional strategies: "Appropriate onsite composition theories, pedagogies, and strategies should be migrated and adapted to the online instructional environment" (Principle 4). F2F techniques based in effective composition theory cannot simply be redeployed for use in the online environment; they must be adapted to suit the modality. For example, Effective Practice 3.5 recommends that "When there is no face-to-face explanatory opportunity and text is the primary means of teaching the writing, [instructors should provide] example strategies for intervening in a clearly written, problem-centered manner" so that online students can better imagine the necessary techniques F2F students acquire through classroom demonstration. Moreover, the modality may present exciting opportunities for alternative methods to deliver some of the best parts of composition pedagogy. For example, Practice 4.2 states, "Teachers [. . .] should employ the interactive potential of digital communications to enable and enact knowledge construction." Because asynchronous online instruction often results in a document trail of interactions in discussion-board posts, wikis, and other forms of shared interaction, the potential exists for students not only to enact knowledge construction but also to study, use, and value that interaction. Thus, while research on computer-mediated and hybrid WAC classes might inform our work, research into effective pedagogy in fully-online WAC courses, guided by the CCCC OWI Position Statement, will be vital as twenty-first century classrooms continue to move into cyberspace. While the Position Statement arises from research in and practitioners from the field of writing studies, these principles can guide online writing instruction across disciplines, as our pedagogical transformations indicate.

## Online Writing-in-the-Disciplines at Eastern Oregon University

Our transformative practice, as well as our participation in summer institute training in August 2011, centers on our university mission to "connect the rural regions of Oregon to a wider world" (Eastern Oregon University, "Mission and Values Statement"). Eastern Oregon University (EOU) is a small, liberal-arts university located in La Grande, Oregon. As of winter quarter 2014, EOU enrolled 3,731 students (FTE=2,471), with just under half of those students fully online (FTE=1,186). In addition to on-campus courses at our main campus in La Grande and online courses, EOU has sixteen regional centers throughout the state of Oregon. These regional centers serve an additional 657 students (FTE=231) in over 45 Oregon counties (EOU, "Institutional Research"). Because Oregon is largely rural, distance education courses, initially correspondence courses and later online and on-site courses have been a substantial component of EOU for over thirty years. EOU currently offers ten fully online four-year bachelor's degrees as well as eighteen fully online minors.

To promote strong writing skill in this geographically dispersed population, EOU has instituted the University Writing Requirement (UWR). The UWR "requires that students receive attention to writing throughout their studies and that students demonstrate their mastery of discipline-specific writing" (EOU, "University Writing Requirement"). To this end, students are required to take the first-year composition course (WR 121: Expository Writing), one lower-level UWR course, and two-upper division UWR courses as specified by their major. UWR course outcomes include a minimum number of written words (both in draft and polished form), attention to discipline-specific conventions, multiple drafts, integration of sources relevant to their discipline and cited appropriately, and attention to peer review and feedback from the instructor at multiple stages of the drafting process.

In spite of EOU's long history with online education and significant focus on writing across the curriculum, faculty professional development in technology for writing purposes has been limited. EOU supports a robust National Writing Project site, but university faculty wanted additional training in instructional technologies. In Summer 2011, a group of faculty came together for the first Summer Institute for Instructional Technology (SIIT), a two-week workshop that investigated best practices in online teaching and learning co-coordinated by Heidi Skurat Harris and Steve Clements. Sixteen participants from across the university participated in the inaugural institute, which centered on California State University-Chico's Rubric for Online Instruction's six components of effective online instruction (see http://www.csuchico.edu/celt/roi/ for more information about the rubric).

As three of these participants—Nancy Knowles (English and Writing), Tawnya Lubbes (Education), and Jacob Harris (Religious Studies)—shared their techniques for effective online instruction, they discovered that effective writing instruction posed some particular challenges in their online classes: promoting student engagement and interaction, helping students navigate the overwhelming amount of reading and writing in the online classroom, and scaffolding and sequencing course activities to help online students complete longer writing assignments effectively.

Although we taught in different content areas at Eastern Oregon University, we also found striking similarities in our transitions between the F2F and online environments. First, we needed to facilitate online learning more intentionally than F2F learning; interacting with students, "being present" in the class, was key to success. This finding is consistent with CCCC OWI Position Statement Effective Practice 3.10, which argues, "Teachers should moderate online class discussions to develop a collaborative OWC and to ensure participation of all students, the free and productive exchange of ideas, and a constant habit of written expression with a genuine audience." Second, multimedia and interactive resources frequently and somewhat counter-intuitively led to better writing. This discovery is consistent with the CCCC OWI Position Statement Effective Practice 3.2, that argues for blending "different and redundant modalities." We discovered that writing *more effectively*, not *more frequently*, achieved University Writing Requirement outcomes. Third, in the online medium, we needed to replace classroom dialogue with shorter written assignments, scaffold larger assignments more clearly, and sequence activities more effectively. This discovery is consistent with CCCC OWI Position Statement Effective Practice

4.1: "When migrating from onsite modalities to the online environment, teachers should break their assignments, exercises, and activities into smaller units to increase opportunities for interaction between teacher and student and among students using both asynchronous and synchronous modalities." In turn, success with these transformations of our writing pedagogy encouraged us to revisit the effectiveness of our F2F classroom practices and use the distance provided by the online modality to realize that F2F students also benefit from the strategies developed for the online environment.

## Translation: Moving Writing Instruction Online

The three instructors who participated in the SIIT 2011, Nancy Knowles (English and Writing), Tawnya Lubbes (Education), and Jacob Harris (Religious Studies) all were tasked with moving writing instruction in their disciplines (practiced not in computer-mediated classrooms or even necessarily in classrooms with robust wireless access) to online modalities. In doing so, they faced challenges in helping students access course content and materials and using those materials effectively. According to Elizabeth Barkley, Professor of Music at Foothill College and author of *Student Engagement Techniques: A Handbook for College Faculty*, only 4% of learners prefer reading as a means of processing information compared to 18% discussion, 27% hands-on learning, and 31% teaching others (139). These figures indicate that access as a component of course delivery is not just a matter of difficulty for those outside the institution, those with hardware limitations, or those with disabilities (Porter 215-16); access is a vital component of the online experience for students attempting to join academic conversations, "those [not] already in the know," (Taylor 133), as the print or text-based modes of interaction may render some conversations inaccessible for particular students.

*Nancy: Reading and Writing as a Barrier to Reading and Writing Online*

When Nancy Knowles, Professor of English and Writing, began teaching literature and technical writing online in 2003, her primary strategy to teach reading and writing was through reading and writing. She simply translated process-writing strategies into the online environment. The online environment revealed limitations of the process approach: at the time, online students had almost no other option for interaction with teachers and peers aside from reading and writing, modes that often failed to replicate the valuable interpersonal collaboration common to the F2F classroom.

Transitioning between F2F and online instruction highlighted problems associated with unexamined emphasis on written text as a means to teach writing and content. Although writing-immersed pedagogy benefits students by encouraging development of literacy skills (Courage 170; Warnock xi), written text may not always be the best access point for students to engage with literate tasks, particularly in an online environment often dominated by written text and particularly for first-year and struggling students for whom reading and writing represent significant challenges. Struggling students manifested a host of problematic behaviors, the most serious of which was simple absence from the online environment. Bombarded with a text-based welcome page, a written syllabus, a dense print textbook or poetry anthology, a bewildering set of folders filled with written lectures and assignment instructions, a discussion board filled with other students apparently capably and confidently posting writing, and later a set of text-based instructor emails asking whether they needed assistance, the path of least resistance was to avoid interaction. Struggling students who attempted to engage did their best to deliver on expectations, producing "safe" posts either vague enough to try to hide confusion or mimicking or outright copying the seemingly successful posts of other students. If they survived the instructor (written) encouragement to improve, they produced mechanical kinds of writing that indicated an ongoing perception of coursework as busywork, not as access to personally enlightening material or professionally beneficial skills. In the online section of WR 320: Technical Writing in Summer 2006, for example, the class average was 67%, which indicates the course could have better served struggling students.

*Jacob: Too Much Writing Online*

Similar to Nancy's text-based approach to enter into reading and writing, Jacob Harris, Instructor in Religious Studies, discovered that F2F discussion did not translate directly into written discussion in his introduction to religion and more advanced religious studies courses. When Jacob first started teaching online in 2006, his experience teaching in the F2F classroom involved his work as a graduate teaching assistant, where senior faculty mentors encouraged long faculty lectures supplemented by shorter discussion groups. When he translated this method to online classes, he found himself telling students to "read the textbook" to replace the lectures and then assigning two discussion questions or prompts each week with two required classmate responses for each question. This method closely replicated the "lecture and discuss" methods from his large F2F religious studies courses.

In addition to replicating this lecture-and-discuss pedagogy, Jacob assumed that students would improve their writing in the discussion forums and in longer written assignments by writing more frequently. However, Jacob found that students, who might have willingly referenced print sources in a F2F classroom, struggled to synthesize such sources in their discussion board posts. Students spent so much time writing weekly discussion posts (the equivalent of two full essays per week) and responding to classmates that they were completing the bare minimum to get by, the quality was rushed and superficial, and they failed to truly engage in discussions with each other. Moreover, because of the massive amount of student writing, Jacob found himself struggling to engage with students on discussion boards to model discussion and highlight relevant course concepts. Writing on discussion boards, in addition to content-writing (such as the twice per term New Religious Experience essays) and readings from the textbook and supplemental readings, meant an overwhelming reading and writing load for students and himself. As a result, his attrition rates hovered around 50% and additional students simply "disappeared" from the class even while still enrolled.

*Tawnya: Need for Scaffolding Online*

Tawnya Lubbes, Assistant Professor of Education, was asked in 2009 to teach a special online section of her Language and Cognition course for a small group of students. This was her first experience with teaching the writing process online. Without realizing the need to transform her F2F course for online delivery, she included PowerPoint presentations to replicate F2F instruction time and discussion boards to replicate in-class discussion. All other course assignments remained as presented F2F, which included weekly reading response guides, drafts of writing assignments, and written reflections. The overarching activity in the course was an in-depth case study of a bilingual informant, including a "thick description" (see Geertz) and an analysis of theoretically salient issues in terms of language acquisition. This activity demanded synthesis, application and evaluative cognitive thinking skills. Students also needed background in the foundations of bilingual education and bilingualism, linguistic analysis, and common miscues of second language learning, and they needed to write analytically using scholarly tone and APA formatting.

To complete this activity in the F2F course, Tawnya placed students into literature and peer editing groups. Students read and revised their writing through a multistep process, submitting their writing in segments and receiving ample feedback to build toward their final drafts. Tawnya provided F2F students examples of previous studies and guided them through the writing process (again reinforcing the need for recursive feedback indicated in OWI Effective Practice 4.1).

Online, Tawnya simply translated elements of the course without transforming them, without scaffolding the information and writing process for the students. She provided PowerPoint presentations without narratives or opportunities for interaction. Discussion questions related to the readings required limited student dialogue. Tawnya encouraged students to complete peer editing or use the Writing Center, but neither activity was required. Because Tawnya did not have time to gather permission from former students to scan and post copies online, examples of the case study were not provided. While she presented a variety of online resources in the CMS, students received little direction for using the resources. While Tawnya identified weekly deadlines, she allowed multiple drafts, even if significantly late. This leniency meant that, rather than moving forward, students spent time rewriting previous work and falling further behind. All in all, the online class produced lower quality case studies than the F2F class. In the F2F class the course average was an 82%, while the online course students averaged 76%. In particular, the online students failed to build upon the background knowledge gained through course readings by connecting the sections of the case study with the chapters from the course text.

While navigating their online writing courses, all three experienced F2F instructors struggled with communicating writing assignments, modeling academic discourse, and giving students the guidance that they needed to complete complex projects and integrate source materials. In the online environment, as Gilliam and Wooten note, students lacked access to the structures that made classroom learning powerful and effective: visual and aural cues, the presence of a reflective practitioner who could informally assess success from moment to moment and adjust delivery to meet student needs, and the physical reality of a community of learners whose presence modeled strategies, provided emotional support, and encouraged questions and deeper thought. Online environments replacing the dynamic of F2F classrooms with inert and overwhelming materials proved to struggling students that college-level work was beyond their capacities.

## Transformation: From Transmission to Engagement

As the instructors faced their failures in their online courses, they each sought to overhaul their online classes in order to more effectively meet the needs of diverse learners who were "separated physically and temporally from their classmates," (Gilliam and Wooten) while struggling to synthesize and integrate new, affectively and cognitively challenging content into their writing.

### *Nancy: Going Native*

In 2009, Nancy began to "go native" (Taylor 139)—that is, to adapt instructional strategies to the students served. To use Porter's words, online access "means starting the writing [or course development] process from audience and working backward to made object [or online course]" (216; see also Savenye, Olina, and Niemczyk). In moving between F2F and online instruction, Nancy discovered multimedia and multi-modal projects as "appropriate strategies" not only "adapted to the online instructional environment," per Practice 4 (CCCC OWI), but also helping in enhancing access to literate learning in all classes.

To serve online students needing access to literate discourse, Nancy broadened the strategies by which she invited student response. At first, she envisioned the daunting task of meeting student needs by knowing them well enough to match their preferences to particular assignments and worried over the fact that learners should also be encouraged to stretch beyond their preferences. But soon, she realized that, as Enujoo Oh and Doohun Lim, researchers in instructional technology at the University of Tennessee, conclude, attempting to match learners to particular assignments was less important than simply providing a variety of access points. Rather than completing one assignment in lockstep with peers, students benefit by options whereby they can self-select the best means to demonstrate skills and knowledge. Nancy's online students responded well to photographing art, clustering, and mapping; using video to capture performances (such as one memorable Bollywood dance routine); and using blogs for interactive public dialogue to stimulate engagement. Creative writing also enhanced emotional and aesthetic engagement with academic writing. Blending media and genres acknowledges that "writing is Technicolor, oral, and thoroughly integrated with visual and audio displays," representing a "secondary literacy" (Diogenes and Lunsford 142), a literacy particularly appropriate to students already learning in an online environment. Using both text and non-text methods of reaching out to students, allowing students to interact visually and aurally through multimedia, opened avenues to writing. Reading and writing operated not as the sole means of communication but as a natural progression from other activities. As a result, the atmosphere and quality of work in Nancy's online courses changed. Students spent time on the discussion board laughing and commiserating over one another's posts, building a classroom community for all participants, not just those confident with text-based forms of communication. Writing produced in these courses became more engaged, more a combination of academic skill and personal interests and therefore more valuable to the students themselves, which ramped up the quality. As an index of the change, the course average for online students enrolled in ENGL 221: Sophomore Seminar in Winter 2013 surpassed that of the on-campus section (85% to 72%).

*Jacob: Fewer, Better Written Assignments*

To transform his online courses and to help students integrate affectively and cognitively difficult source material in discussion board posts and writing assignments, Jacob scaled back the number of required discussion board postings from two posts every week to one post every two weeks. In a 2007 study, Wang and Woo found that online students have more time to "think, clarify, and respond" to their classmates and can rely more heavily on using sources and other materials to support themselves than they can in F2F discussions (281), but because of the more time-consuming nature of the written discussion, the online discussion time-frame needed to be much longer (284). Thus, online discussions can help students improve their synthesis and research skills but only when students are not overwhelmed with a multitude of text- or print-based reading and writing activities. The "less is more" philosophy also applies to instructor texts where concision aids in avoiding confusion (Ragain and White 406).

In alternating activity weeks, Jacob supplemented text-based sources with videos and audio recordings in which adherents of a variety of religions discussed their experiences in those religious traditions, which aligns with CCCC OWI Effective Practice 3.2 "Text-based instruction should be supplemented with oral and/or video instruction in keeping with the need for presenting instruction in different and redundant modalities." In discussion boards, students synthesized concepts from the textbook with the experiences of those who practiced the religions they were studying and theories posed by religious studies scholars. Just as Nancy incorporated audio, video, and kinesthetic activities as a way of differentiating instruction to make literate conversations accessible, Jacob incorporated these tools as an entrance to difficult scholarly discussions about the secular, academic study of religion.

Besides requiring fewer posts, Jacob clarified the requirements for discussion boards and encouraged students to include their own experiences as well as synthesizing sources. George Collison, Bonnie Elbaum, Sarah Haavind, and Robert Tinker, authors of *Facilitating Online Learning: Effective Strategies for Moderators,* reinforce these practices, suggesting that a healthy online discussion has clearly defined expectations and reminders of those expectations in the directions for each board (78-80). They further advise that discussion boards encourage deep dialogue where participants think critically about content (140). After the changes to the discussion board criteria, students in Jacob's religious studies classes spent more time in deep dialogue with their classmates. And, just as Warnock recommends (79), this deep dialogue constituted a significant portion (30%) of the course grade. In addition to dialogue in discussion boards, students interacted with each other to complete group projects in all of his online classes, further integrating course concepts and personal experiences while interacting with each other.

During his discussions with students, Jacob also transformed the focus of his feedback from end-of-discussion summative assessments to formative assessment. Instead of waiting until the end of the week to identify an excellent comment or post, fewer discussion boards meant that Jacob had more time to participate during class discussion, pointing out excellent student input in the flow of discussion. This practice conforms to OWI Effective Practice 3.5 regarding instructors' role in guiding improvement: "When there is no face-to-face explanatory opportunity and text is the primary means of teaching the writing, example strategies for intervening in a clearly written, problem-centered manner include ... modeling by writing at the level that is being required of the student and providing doable tasks with instructions" (CCCC OWI).

In addition to including discussion board rubrics, samples of both adequate and insufficient posts, and discussion of the problems with insufficient posts, Jacob supported student success by modeling the discourse he asked of students. He followed his own rules, incorporating outside sources, passages of the textbook, and authentic leading questions. As a result of this guidance, Jacob's students not only synthesized sources more clearly in discussion board posts, but they also transferred those writing skills to longer written texts, such as the New Religious Experience assignment where students analyze an unfamiliar religious ritual. In addition, student attrition rates dropped to around 30% and those students enrolled in the course were more likely to complete more of the assignments and successfully complete the class.

*Tawnya: Scaffolding Online Student Work*

Transitioning between F2F and online instruction not only emphasized the need for Tawnya to improve student interaction and incorporate multimedia elements to support print-based materials but also revealed the need to scaffold and sequence course assignments so that online students could complete tasks without synchronous or real-time direction from faculty. OWI **Effective Practice 4.1 identifies the need for instructors to** "break their assignments, exercises, and activities into smaller units to increase opportunities for interaction between teacher and student and among students using both asynchronous and synchronous modalities" (CCCC OWI). In addition to online scaffolding, Tawnya incorporated peer review in online classes. Miky Ronan and Dorothy Langley, authors of "Scaffolding Complex Tasks by Open Online Submission: Emerging Patterns and Profiles," incorporate student review and commentary in their "open online submission," where students submit parts of writing at various stages for other students and faculty to review. This process not only assists students in understanding the task but also permits instructors to identify communication problems and intervene (58). Because peer review requires risk-taking in sharing documents, it has the potential to build trust necessary to form a learning community comprised of multiple and valued perspectives in the manner that F2F courses do.

After evaluating the pitfalls of simply translating the course from F2F to online, Tawnya modified the course to integrate all four of the scaffolding strategies that Michael Hannafin, Susan Land and Kevin Oliver's "Open Learning Environments: Foundations, Methods, and Models" identifies: 1) procedural scaffolds to help give and clarify directions, 2) conceptual scaffolds that guide learners into working through multiple concepts, 3) metacognitive scaffolds that prompt students to look at the subject from multiple perspectives, and 4) strategic scaffolds, including alternative approaches to planning and application processes.

Procedural scaffolds included the reorganization of the course structure. Outside resources appeared in units that corresponded with each section of the case study. The revised course also scheduled regular due dates in order to keep the students on track. In creating conceptual scaffolds, she realigned textbook chapters to match the specific sections of the case study as students completed them. Metacognitive and strategic scaffolds included collaborative learning groups and the requirement that students submit reviews of work and summaries of the students' editing group progress. Some of this peer interaction occurred within the Blackboard™ CMS in order to allow Tawnya to facilitate and monitor the progress, providing the instructor intervention and support that Carla Garnam and Robert Kaleta, published in *Teaching with Technology Today,* deem necessary to help students manage their time and expectations. In addition, she designed discussion board prompts to ask higher-order questions (see Collison et al. and Warnock) and to assist students in developing inquiry methods to gather information for their case studies. Tawnya also modified PowerPoint™ presentations to include instructor notes and summaries. In presenting the case study assignment, she worked from whole to part and part to whole, providing the big picture of the case study (including individual case studies completed by previous students) and then breaking that picture down into units that integrated all four scaffolding strategies.

As a result of her efforts, students in the second online version of the course produced some of the best quality case studies Tawnya had ever seen, all while meeting the course objectives. Students in this course moved from the previous 76% average to an 89% average in the transformed course section. Positive written and verbal feedback from the students confirmed success. One student stated: "I learned a lot of new stuff and it was good to finally be able to use everything we have learned. I am so glad we had sections of our case study due throughout the term." Another student advised: "the breaking down of the final paper into sections was particularly helpful for successfully completing the course." Further, Tawnya was able to share her course redesign with her colleagues who taught the same course in online and hybrid formats.

By transforming their instruction to better support online learners, Nancy, Jacob, and Tawnya achieved noticeable improvements in students' academic performance. The application of multi-media and multimodal projects and a broadening of strategies and access points in their courses allowed for learners to meet their course objectives without the struggle in communicating via one-dimensional procedural writing. Scaffolding, clear guiding directions, increased frequency of interactions, and instructional design that was less text-driven and more focused on visuals, including video and audio recordings, greatly contributed to the successes the instructors observed in their courses. The three also recognized that specific grading criteria with frequent feedback mechanisms assisted the students in understanding and meeting the course requirements. Through these strategies, online students became more engaged with course materials and activities and more successful in demonstrating acquired knowledge and skills.

## Taking It Back: Energizing the Face-to-Face Classroom with Online Strategies

While the CCCC OWI Position Statement addresses the need to transform pedagogy when moving from the F2F to the online environment, it doesn't address the impact of online instruction on F2F instruction. As increasing numbers of recursive practitioners teach in both modalities, they may find the online teaching experience informing their F2F practice. Once Nancy, Jacob, and Tawnya saw student improvement in their online courses, they began to take back lessons from those courses to their F2F classes.

### *Nancy and Jacob: More Productive Use of Multimedia and F2F Class Time*

Expanding Nancy's repertoire of online delivery methods has reinforced the necessity of access in the F2F setting. In online teaching, "seat time" is replaced by time engaged in meaningful course activities. This experience helped Nancy re-envision her use of F2F class time as devoted to productive hands-on work. In writing classes, rather than attempting to cover one element of writing everyone in the class needs to practice (which is not possible), Nancy usually spends the beginning of the week in interactive activities and devotes the end of the week to writing time, coaching, and response to drafts—freeing students to work individually or in small groups on the aspect of writing that most needs their attention. Nancy also finds technology playing an increased role in her F2F classroom, as Blackboard becomes a repository for drafts and a place for peer review.

Jacob's F2F practice now benefits from his online use of multimedia and discussion strategies. Students in his F2F Introduction to Religion course, for example, create their own religion as a final synthesis activity, giving F2F presentations and also compiling supplementary online resources. Modeling academic discourse and discussion has become the focus of Jacob's classes. Unlike the lecture courses Jacob delivered as a graduate student, he now asks students to give mini-presentations on course material, complete daily "check-in" writing, and he provides guidance and feedback in active discussion with the students. CCCC OWI Effective Practice 3.10, which states that "Teachers should moderate online class discussions to develop a collaborative OWC and to ensure participation of all students, the free and productive exchange of ideas, and a constant habit of written expression with a genuine audience" not only transformed his online pedagogy but his F2F pedagogy as well, helping him to overcome the restrictive "lecture and discuss" methods of his graduate training.

Jacob's and Nancy's transitions between F2F and online instruction also demonstrate that multimedia and active learning facilitate writing. Both classrooms provide students new means of synthesizing difficult course content thorough hands-on and collaborative activities. Writing resulted from these practices more organically, becoming a part of the course as a result of, and in some cases in response to, the visual, auditory, and kinesthetic experiences students encountered in their classes.

In addition, both Nancy and Jacob addressed the affective element of transitioning from personal to scholarly writing. For Nancy, multimedia and active learning helped students overcome anxieties associated with writing by connecting with topics, developing a deep reservoir of ideas, and even producing outstanding personal writing before turning to academic writing, armed with the interest, ideas, and sentences. In Jacob's religion courses, he struggled with ardent believers' affective responses to the secular academic study of religion, encountering perspectives through a non-faith-based lens as they studied as "critics not caretakers" (McCutcheon). The use of multimedia in both F2F and online classes allowed students to witness adherents of various faiths discuss their beliefs and helped students stimulate various parts of the brain, enhancing the creation of new neural networks to process difficult scholarly criticism (Costa and Nuhfer) and moving from defenses of their own faith practices into open consideration of the practices of other faiths, moving them effectively toward higher affective domain competencies.

### *Tawnya: Improved F2F Scaffolding*

Because of the success of the revised online course, Tawnya integrated the new strategies of scaffolding into the F2F classroom. She provided an overview of the case study at the beginning of the course and then broke the instruction and course readings down into units. Each unit then corresponded to a section of the paper that the students would write and revise, thus providing the necessary references and support for each section. Additionally, Tawnya redesigned the peer editing groups to employ a writer's workshop format where each individual was responsible for a component of the editing process each week (see Armstrong and Paulson). During the peer review process, she also required regular progress reports. Tawnya, like Nancy and Jacob, used the online platform as a place to store unit resources, rubrics and other course documents for the F2F classroom. Finally, the Blackboard Grade Center™ was integrated into the F2F class in order to track progress. These modifications of the

F2F class improved student writing quality and consistency in meeting course outcomes. Most importantly, just as Armstrong and Paulson predicted, Tawnya found the course easier to deliver, and students provided positive feedback about the learning process.

As increasing numbers of faculty members across disciplines—like Nancy, Jacob, and Tawnya—teach in both the F2F and online environments, we can expect increased reflections on the intersections between teaching modalities. It seems obvious that the online classroom would translate strategies from the F2F classroom into the online environment because the F2F classroom came first. In addition, as the CCCC OWI Position Statement and this research indicate, faculty members must not only translate but transform those strategies to meet the needs of online learners. Perhaps even more interesting is the swirling occurring not only among students enrolling in courses employing a variety of modalities but also among faculty members teaching a wide range of technology-enhanced courses, from traditional F2F courses with a CMS repository of materials to courses housed fully online in the CMS environment. As faculty members swirl, their professional development will should naturally take lessons learned in the online modality back to the F2F classroom, and those lessons may in turn transform the F2F classroom. Based on the experiences of Nancy, Jacob, and Tawnya, the movement from online to F2F modalities suggests particular benefits to swirling: because the online environment distances faculty members from the culture of their F2F classrooms, teaching online can help them better perceive the quality of F2F delivery. In addition, online instruction demands more explicit scaffolding simply because instructors are not physically present to ad-lib instruction. Thus, online instruction becomes a "sandbox" for imagining explicit media, scaffolding, and use of class time that might also enhance F2F instruction.

## Translation, Transformation, Taking It Back: Concluding Thoughts

With the rise in popularity of online courses, many universities are increasing their online or hybrid offerings to "keep up with the continuing population growth and demands for lifelong learning" (Bleed qtd. in Young A34). Increased demand for online courses obligates faculty to transform their F2F strategies for the electronic environment so that all students can access learning, but increased online teaching loads also provide a unique opportunity as part of reflective practice to take newly re-imagined strategies back to the F2F classroom. Our individual experiences, combined with insights from the CCCC OWI Position Statement of Principles and Example Effective Practices for Online Writing Instruction, provide a starting point for faculty seeking to undergo similar transformational practices and for further research into the effectiveness of these particular practices in relation to WAC anywhere on the F2F-online spectrum. Key conclusions include the following principles.

> Students need the opportunity to learn from a variety of media (*Effective Practice* 3.2).

Because communication in online courses still relies mainly on writing, as Nancy's and Jacob's experiences indicate, online students need fewer, better written assignments, combined with multimedia texts and the chance to demonstrate learning through multimedia options. Similarly, when we take this learning from the online "sandbox" back to the F2F classroom, we must recognize that while F2F students have more opportunities for interpersonal interaction in the classroom, they, too, benefit from multimedia pathways to writing and opportunities to "write" using multimedia tools. Additional research on the effectiveness of using multi-modal elements should be conducted to understand the specific relationships between multi-modal instruction and increased writing competencies across the curriculum.

> Students need models and scaffolding (*Effective Practice* 3.5 and 4.1).

Because online students lack F2F opportunities to hear instructors discuss writing assignments and answer questions about them and because putting questions into writing requires more student effort, online students need models and explanatory activities—such as those outlined in Effective Practice 3.5, including instructions and questions, and those provided by Michael Hannafin, Susan Land and Kevin Oliver—to better comprehend assignments and difficult concepts. For example, when Tawnya needed students to incorporate an understanding of bilingualism, linguistic analysis, and second language miscues into their case studies, including sequenced examples and scaffolding, instruction helped students work through complex content-area synthesis and produce better writing. When Jacob needed to help his students move beyond lower-order affective reactions and more complex interactions with religious studies theory, he modeled the discourse he expected his students to achieve. As Effective Practice 4.1 indicates, scaffolding and modeling not only build student understanding but also enhance interactions among teacher and students. As students receive more frequent peer and instructor feedback on smaller assignments, they experience less isolation and more engagement. While F2F students receive ongoing feedback from their peers and instructor through classroom interaction, they also find models and scaffolding activities beneficial. In this way, using online instruction as a "sandbox" can assist reflective practitioners in developing more precise supports to make learning accessible for all students. Additional research in this area could include examining the relationship between various types of scaffolding and modeling practices and students' abilities to enter academic discourse communities.

> Students need faculty presence and disciplinary community (*Effective Practice* 3.10 and 4.2).

In the process of better serving online students, Nancy, Jacob, and Tawnya became more active on the discussion board. Tawnya and Jacob, in particular, found themselves using discussion boards for more in-depth student engagement as well as to demonstrate student mastery of course concepts. As Effective Practice 3.10 observes, instructor collaboration with students in discussion boards "ensure[s] participation of all students, the free and productive exchange of ideas, and a constant habit of written expression with a genuine audience." Providing interactive spaces for students helped to mitigate some of the isolation issues online students experience in being distant both spatially and temporally from each other and from the instructor. Even in the F2F environment, students need to experience faculty members as present, as collaborators in a discourse community that includes students. After all, the heart of successful WAC efforts is helping students develop new knowledge bases constructively. Using the online "sandbox" to explore course dialogue as disciplinary community-building encourages F2F faculty members to transform "seat time," as all three faculty members did, into opportunities for the active practice of knowledge construction, building the discourse communities necessary to support students in navigating the unfamiliar terrain of new texts, research methods and theories in our disciplines. While a number of studies across the disciplines have examined effective practices in using discussion boards, among other collaborative strategies, more work needs to be done with the relationship between faculty interaction and student engagement in these online spaces, and in building disciplinary discourse communities through classroom dialogue.

The remarkable consistency across the teaching practice of the faculty authors involved in this project, who have a total of thirty years of combined online teaching experience, reflects the need for all faculty to pause and consider the moves they make while immigrating from the "home country" of the F2F classroom into foreign territory of online education and also when returning home, equipped with new perspectives. And as we transform our courses, we transform ourselves as teachers, and ultimately, as lifelong learners.

## Notes

1. Some research from outside the field of rhetoric and composition has also been conducted and upholds the need for engagement in WAC courses, indicating that engaged

students who participated in discussion boards and received feedback from the instructor were more likely to be successful in classes (Defazio, Jones, Tennant, and Hook).

**Works Cited**

Allen, Elaine I. and Jeff Seaman. "Changing Course: Ten Years of Tracking Online Education in the United States." Babson Survey Research Group. 2013. Web. 21 Oct. 2014.

Armstrong, Sonya and Eric Paulson. "Whither Peer Review? Terminology Matters for the Writing Classroom." *Teaching English at the Two Year College* 35.4 (2008): 398-407. Print.

Barkley, Elizabeth F. *Student Engagement Techniques: A Handbook for College Faculty.* San Francisco: Jossey-Bass, 2009. Print.

California State University-Chico (CSU-Chico). "What Does a High-Quality Online Course Look Like?" California State University-Chico Rubric for Online Instruction. n.d. Web. 10 February 2012.

Chadwick, Scott and Jon Dorbolo. "Inter-Quest: Designing a Communication-Intensive Web-Based Course." In Reiss, Selfe, and Young. 118-28.

Collison, George, Bonnie Elbaum, Sarah Haavind, and Robert Tinker. *Facilitating Online Learning: Effective Strategies for Moderators.* Madison, WI: Atwood Publishing 2000. Print.

Conference on College Composition and Communication (CCCC). "Establishing a Statement of Principles for Online Writing Instruction (OWI)." 9 April 2013. Web. 20 April 2014.

—. "A Position Statement of Principles and Example Effective Practices for Online Writing Instruction." 13 November 2013. Web. 21 Oct. 2014.

Costa, Maria and Ed Nuhfer. "Psychomotor Domain: How We Learn Physical Skills Can Teach Us Something." California State University-Los Angeles and California State University-Channel Islands. 10 February 2012. Web. 21 Oct. 2014.

Courage, Richard. "Asynchronicity: Delivering Composition and Literature in the Cyberclassroom." Yancey 168-82.

Dean, Christopher. "Developing and Assessing an Online Research Course." *Across the Disciplines 6.* 19 Jan. 2009. Web. 21 Oct. 2014.

Defazio, Joseph, Josette Jones, Felisa Tennant, and Sarah Anne Hook. "Academic Literacy: The Importance and Impact of Writing Across the Curriculum—A Case Study." *Journal of the Scholarship of Teaching and Learning* 10.2 (June 2010): 34-47. Print.

Diogenes, Marvin, and Andrea A. Lunsford. "Toward Delivering New Definitions of Writing." Yancey 141-54.

—. "Institutional Research." N.d. Web. 29 Jan. 2014.

—. "Mission and Values Statement." Office of the President. February 3, 2004. Web.

—. "University Writing Requirement." N.d. Web.

Garnam, Carla and Robert Kaleta. "Introduction to Hybrid Courses." *Teaching with Technology Today* 8.6 (2002). 10 February 2012. Web.
Geertz, Clifford. *The Interpretation of Cultures*. New York: Basic Books Publishing, 2000. Print.
Gibson, Keith and Beth Hewett. "Annotated Bibliography: CCCC Committee on Best Practices in Online Writing Instruction." N.d. Web.
Gilliam, Ken and Shannon Wooten. "Re-embodying Online Composition: Ecologies of Writing in Unreal Time and Space." *Computers and Composition Online*. Spring 2014. Web.
Hannafin, Michael, Susan Land and Kevin Oliver. "Open Learning Environments: Foundations, Methods, and Models." *Instructional Design Theories and Models: A New Paradigm of Instructional Theory*. Ed. C. M. Reigeluth. vol. II. Mahwah, NJ: Erlbaum, 1999. 115-140. Print.
Hewett, Beth and Christa Ehmann. *Preparing Educators for Online Writing Instruction: Principles and Processes*. Urbana: NCTE, 2004. Print.
Hewett, Beth. *The Online Writing Conference*. Heineman: Portsmouth, NH, 2011.
Lowes, Susan. "Online Teaching and Classroom Change: The Trans-classroom Teacher in the Age of the Internet." *Innovate* 4.3: (2008). 10 February 2012. Web.
Lundsford, Karen J. ed. "Writing Technologies and Writing Across the Disciplines: Current Lessons and Future Trends." *Across the Disciplines*. January 19, 2009. Web.
McCutcheon, Russell T. *Critics not Caretakers: Redescribing the Public Study of Religion*. Albany: SUNY University Press, 2001. Print.
Neff, Joyce Magnotto, and Carl Whithaus. *Writing Across Distances and Disciplines: Research and Pedagogy in Distributed Learning*. New York: Lawrence Erlbaum, 2008.
Oh, Eunjoo, and Doohun Lim. "Cross Relationships between Cognitive Styles and Learner Variables in Online Learning Environment." *Journal of Interactive Online Learning* 4.1 (Summer 2005): 53-66.
Palmquist, Michael. "A Brief History of Computer-Support for Writing Centers and Writing-Across-the Curriculum Programs." *Computers and Composition* 20.4 (2003): 395-413. 4 June 2012. Web.
Palloff, Rena, and Keith Pratt. *Building Online Learning Communities*. San Francisco: Jossey-Bass, 2007. Print.
Porter, James E. "Recovering Delivery for Digital Rhetoric." *Computers & Composition* 26.4 (2009): 207-224. *Academic Search Premier*. 7 June 2012. Web.
Ragan, Tillman J., and Patricia R. White. "What We Have Here Is a Failure to Communicate: The Criticality of Writing in Online Instruction." *Computers and Composition* 18 (2001): 399-409. Print.
Reiss, Donna, Dickie Selfe, and Art Young. *Electronic Communication Across the Curriculum*. WAC Clearinghouse. Spring 1998. Web.

Ronan, Miky, and Dorothy Langley. "Scaffolding Complex Tasks by Open Online Submission: Emerging Patterns and Profiles." *Journal of Asynchronous Learning Networks* 8:4 (2004). 39-61. 18 June 2012. Web.

Savenye, Wilhelmina C., Zane Olina, and Mary Niemczyk. "So You Are Going to Be an Online Writing Instructor: Issues in Designing, Developing, and Delivering an Online Course." *Computers and Composition* 18.4 (2001): 371-85. *ERIC.* 7 June 2012. Web.

Thaiss, Chris, and Tara Porter. " The State of WAC/WID in 2010: Methods and Results of the U.S. Survey of the International WAC/WID Mapping Project." *College Composition and Communication* 61.3 (February 2010). 534-570. Print.

Taylor, Todd. "Design, Delivery, and Narcolepsy." Yancey 127-40.

Wang, Qiyun, and Huay Lit Woo. "Systematic Planning for ICT Integration in Topic Learning." *Educational Technology & Society* 10.1 (2007): 148-156. Web.

Warnock, Scott. *Teaching Writing Online.* Urbana: NCTE, 2009. Print.

Yancey, Kathleen Blake, ed. *Delivering College Composition: The Fifth Canon.* Poetsmouth, NH: Boynton/Cook, 2006. Print.

Young, Jeffrey. "'Hybrid' teaching seeks to end the divide between traditional and online instruction." *The Chronicle of Higher Education* 48.28 (2002): A33-34. 10 February 2012. Web.

# Review

## JUSTIN NICHOLES

Schreiber, Brooke R., Eunjeong Lee, Jennifer T. Johnson, and Norah Fahim, eds. (2022). *Linguistic Justice on Campus: Pedagogy and Advocacy for Multilingual Students*. Multilingual Matters. 235 pages, including index.

Those of us in writing studies and its movements, such as writing across the curriculum (WAC), have long benefited from colleagues reminding us of the ways writing and language assessment in effect measures exposure to or inclination to employ dialects of English in the United States closest to what many White Americans use: White mainstream English. The Conference on College Composition and Communication (CCCC), for instance, released in 2009 and reaffirmed in 2014 the CCCC Statement on Second Language Writing and Writers, which urged such practical steps as assessing writing not at mechanical levels only, but at rhetorical levels additionally. Looking beyond prescriptive grammar is done so as not to penalize writers whose linguistic resources are multiple.

Leaders of the field's antiracist efforts, notably Asao B. Inoue (2014, 2015, 2019, 2021), too have theorized the unjust consequences of holding students accountable to White mainstream English in classroom settings. Supportive empirical studies have begun to quantify the statistically significantly higher burden (i.e., quantifiable operationalizations of linguistic injustice) placed on multilingual writers engaging with English for academic writing and publishing (Hanauer & Englander, 2011; Hanauer et al., 2019). While we have evidence that grades become affectively significant—material students seize upon to construct academic identities as *belonging*, or not, in college (Inman & Powell, 2018)—we also have evidence that assessment (I argue) needs to be radically reimagined sooner or later. What are we waiting for?

An important advancement toward answering this question can be found in the book under review here. A survey of relevant academic landscapes and of what is at stake concerning the issue of linguistic justice on campus appears here in *Linguistic Justice on Campus: Pedagogy and Advocacy for Multilingual Students* (2022), edited by Brooke R. Schreiber, Eunjeong Lee, Jennifer T. Johnson, and Norah Fahim. This book enters our fields' conversations not only at a time when our grappling with how to create (and to justify to our colleagues the value of) methods of just assessment continues to intensify—but also at a time of significant suffering in the United States. A pandemic has led not only to disparate levels of disease and death, but also to resurgences in brazen and public displays of hate (such as those aimed at our Asian family), insurrection, and political movements hellbent on undermining trust in democratic processes.

The book begins with Chapter 1, "Introduction: Why Linguistic Justice, and Why Now?", in which Eunjeong Lee, Jennifer T. Johnson, and Brooke R. Schreiber succinctly identify the need for books like this one: "Despite [...] theory-building, in practice, writing classrooms and other campus spaces are still dominated by a deficit and racist perspective toward language-minoritized students" (p. 1). Lee, Johnson, and Schreiber refer to anti-Asian hate spewed anew from White nationalists and scapegoating politicians, as well as hate embodied by travel bans and deportation threats made to children whose parents traveled to the United States (like many, if not all, of our White settler ancestors did) in hopes of better lives. After identifying justice as a process, the editor-authors call on us to join them in efforts to "create an unapologetically inclusive, accessible and humanizing writing ecology where multilingual students can amplify their voices" (p. 13). Toward this end, the book is described as comprising three main parts: Part 1: Translingual and Antidiscriminatory Pedagogy and Practices (Chapters 2-5); Part 2: Advocacy in the Writing Center (Chapters 6-9); and Part 3: Professional Development (Chapters 10-12). As a coda, Shawna Shapiro provides Chapter 13, "Afterword," generously synthesizing the conversation and making poignant calls to action.

Part 1: Translingual and Antidiscriminatory Pedagogy and Practices begins with Chapter 2, "Locating Linguistic Justice in Language Identity Surveys," in which Shanti Bruce, Rebecca Lorimer Leonard, and Deirdre Vinyard report findings from a mixed-methods study that, at its heart, highlights inherent limitations of many surveys used in higher education to sort students linguistically. Their results, derived from survey data ($N = 1,870$) and focus-group results ($n = 32$), suggest students frequently perform themselves in interviews in ways that subvert the limitations of institutional labels, such as "second language writer" or "monolingual writer" (p. 27). Importantly, the authors warn that "in supplying to students the available discourse, surveys may perpetuate the monolingual ideologies that they may have sought to move beyond" (p. 32). In Chapter 3, "Autoethnographic Performance of Difference as Antiracist Pedagogy," Zhaozhe Wang provides a very excellent writing-assignment prompt for autoethnography as a research approach. Case-study reporting suggests that any student, no matter their linguistic background, may hold monolingual ideologies and perform themselves in their writing with language indexing linguistic practices normalizing White mainstream English. In Chapter 4, "Dis/Locating Linguistic Terrorism: Writing American Indian Languages Back Into the Rhetoric Classroom," Rachel Presley explores "geographically emplaced decolonial work and the ways in which future rhetoricians may reorient the field toward (alter)Native sovereignties" (p. 59). This chapter presents specific activities and resources writing instructors can use to raise awareness of occupied landscapes we harvest resources from every day. In the final chapter in Part 1, Chapter 5, "Audience Awareness, Multilingual Realities: Child Language Brokers in the First Year Writing Classroom," Kaia L. Simon reminds us that the United States has always in reality been multilingual—despite monolingual ideologies governing expectations and practices in language assessment. To illustrate, Simon draws from a case study of 25 Hmong women with experiences of language brokering for their families, and the rhetorical potential these participants' experiences can provide for all students in first-year writing classrooms.

Moving from general classroom practices to a central institution and possible WAC as well as linguistic-justice vehicle, the writing center, the book moves to Part 2: Advocacy in the Writing Center. Here, in Chapter 6, "Valuing Language Diversity Through Translingual Reading Groups in the Writing Center," Sharada Krishnamurthy, Celeste Del Russo, and Donna Mehalchick-Opal report results from reading-group discussion analysis and client report forms. Importantly, the authors argue that writing centers largely "continue to uphold monolingual standards of language use and implicit bias against language diversity in the tutoring context" (p. 92). The authors' analysis of their data led to conclusions that tutors indicated that, as a result of training, they increased their awareness of translanguaging and translingual practices. In Chapter 7, "Beyond Welcoming Acceptance: Re-Envisioning Consultant Education and Writing Center Practices Toward Social Justice for Multilingual Writers," Hidy Basta analyzes response papers written by writing consultants to locate indications of conceptual shifts away from monolingual ideologies that normalize White mainstream English. The chapter also touches on the tension consultants may experience while struggling to honor linguistic performance seemingly different from White mainstream English and to help students navigate professors who take points off students' writing for such differences. In Chapter 8, "Embracing Difficult Conversations: Making Antiracist and Decolonial Writing Center Programming Visible," Marilee Brooks-Gillies verbalizes this tension between theory and outside expectations, arguing that writing centers not only need to change from the inside, but also need to begin the work of challenging notions that writing centers are institutions that correct and maintain monolingual ideologies and practices. In Brooks-Gillies' words, "As we change from the inside, we can move that change outward into our campus communities" (p. 135). In Chapter 9, "Social (Justice) Media: Advocating for Multilingual Writers in a Multimodal World," Emma Catherine Perry and Paula Rawlins likewise consider how changes in the writing center can impact structures outside it. They document a social-media effort to share antiracist pedagogy, such as pedagogy related to translingualism and linguistic diversity, to wider audiences.

Finally, in Part 3: Professional Development, the book continues with Chapter 10, "Combatting Monolingualism Through Rhetorical Listening: A Faculty Workshop," in which Alexandra Watkins and Lindsey Ives detail professional-development events that invite introspection meant to challenge implicitly held monolingualism. Here again, important wrestling with goals is explored: When, if at all, does one help students who may wish, for whatever reasons, for their writing to approximate mechanical and rhetorical moves associated with White mainstream English? In Chapter 11, "*Grassroots* Professional Development: Engaging Multilingual Identities and Expansive Literacies Through Pedagogical-Cultural Historical Activity (PCHAT) and Translingualism," Cristina Sánchez-Martín and Joyce R. Walker consider the important topic of multilingual graduate teachers of writing. Reporting qualitative data provided by Sánchez-Martín, the chapter emphasizes the importance of programmatic conditions promoting "expansive languaging and writing practices in line with translingual and CHAT-informed paradigms, which foster social justice" (p. 195). Finally, in Part 3's Chapter 12, "Looking Beyond Grammar Deficiencies: Moving Faculty in Economics Toward a Difference-as-Resource Pedagogical Paradigm," Kendon Kurzer presents literature review-supported pedagogical suggestions meant to challenge monolingual norms and de facto racist conditions in economics-classroom settings and beyond.

A significant gem within this book is Chapter 13, "Afterword," in which Shawna Shapiro crystallizes three particularly central questions emerging from this book: the question of (a) how to leverage linguistic diversity as a resource, (b) how to realize linguistic justice for multilingual and multidialectical writers, and (c) how to be successful at doing the above. Personally, as a teacher-scholar who wishes to do good things as an ardent advocate for multilingual writers, I found Shapiro's discussion of how we might rhetorically approach colleagues especially valuable. In Shapiro's words, "One concern not talked about enough in conversations about social justice education is that the *discourse we use* to frame this work may obscure opportunities for connection with others who share many of our goals but who describe their work differently" (p. 221). Shapiro's suggestions that we use our rhetorical training to approach audiences, who may be more or less likely to resist frameworks such as social justice or linguistic diversity, to gather support seem especially valuable.

Strengths of the book include the many chapters presenting frameworks for the problem of persistent deficit models of languaging in higher education and beyond. Herein, a teacher-scholar whose work intersects with issues of linguistic justice (and whose doesn't/couldn't?) will find valuable presentations of what is at stake for multilingual writers. The book, though, has its limitations—as all works of scholarship do. Often, instead of qualitative claims matching the type of evidence being presented, unhedged quantitative cause-effect or association-type claims, about complex and sometimes un-operationalized theoretical concepts, too often seem to appear. Rigorous, replicable methods to address complex social issues surely can help, as Shapiro similarly argues in the afterword, broaden how we approach potentially resistant audiences for the sake of our multilingual community. Being clear about what we do and do not believe to be the case, and the evidence and methods we use to conclude this, can also help point future researchers in productive directions.

People who would benefit from reading this book include, primarily, writing instructors and program directors in higher education in the United States. Secondary audiences include anyone who has a say in how higher education evaluates the writing and language assessed in classrooms. This book is a valuable, ethical, and compassionate contribution to the field of writing studies. We owe it to our communities to keep pushing against monolingual models that frame linguistic variation from White mainstream English as a deficit and assessment practices that penalize multilingualism while rewarding monolingualism.

## References

*Conference on College Composition and Communication (CCCC).* (2009/2014). *CCCC Statement on Second Language Writing and Writers.* Retrieved from http://www.ncte.org/cccc/resources/positions/secondlangwriting.

Hanauer, D. I., & Englander, K. (2011). Quantifying the burden of writing research articles in a second language: Data from Mexican scientists. *Written Communication, 28*(4), 403-416. https://doi.org/10.1177/0741088311420056

Hanauer, D. I., Sheridan, C. L., & Englander, K. (2019). Linguistic injustice in the writing of research articles in English as a second language: Data from Taiwanese and Mexican researchers. *Written Communication, 36*(1), 136-154. https://doi.org/10.1177/0741088318804821

Inman, J. O., & Powell, R. A. (2018). In the absence of grades: Dissonance and desire in course-contract classrooms. *College Composition and Communication, 70*(1), 30-56.

Inoue, A. B. (2014). Theorizing failure in U.S. writing assessments. *Research in the Teaching of English, 48*(3), 330-352.

Inoue, A. B. (2015). *Antiracist writing assessment ecologies: Teaching and assessing writing for a socially just future.* The WAC Clearinghouse; Parlor Press.

Inoue, A. B. (2019). *Labor-based grading contracts: Building equity and inclusion in the compassionate writing classroom.* The WAC Clearinghouse. https://wac.colostate.edu/books/perspectives/labor/

Inoue, A. B. (2021). *Above the well: An antiracist literacy argument from a boy of color.* The WAC Clearinghouse.

# Contributors

**Letizia Guglielmo** is Professor of English and Interdisciplinary Studies at Kennesaw State University and Faculty Success Fellow with the Center for Excellence in Teaching and Learning. Her writing and research explore feminist rhetoric and pedagogy, gender and pop culture, and professional development for students and faculty. Publications include *Immigrant Scholars in Rhetoric, Composition, and Communication: Memoirs of a First Generation*, *Misogyny in American Culture: Causes, Trends, Solutions*, *Scholarly Publication in a Changing Academic Landscape*, *Contingent Faculty Publishing in Community: Case Studies for Successful Collaborations*, and *MTV and Teen Pregnancy: Critical Essays on 16 and Pregnant* and *Teen Mom*.

**Judson Kidd**, EdS, is a middle grades social studies teacher and department chair at Fulton County Public Schools in Atlanta, Georgia. He is currently working toward earning his doctoral degree at Kennesaw State University. His research explores social studies curriculum and global citizenship education.

**Dominique McPhearson** holds a BS in Integrative Studies with a concentration in writing from Kennesaw State University.

**Elisabeth L. Miller** is Assistant Professor of English, Director of the Writing and Speaking Initiative, and Director of the Writing and Speaking in the Disciplines program at the University of Nevada, Reno. She researches and teaches about writing across the curriculum, and disability and literacy. Her work appears in venues including *College English*, *Across the Disciplines*, *Rhetoric of Health and Medicine*, *Written Communication*, and her book *What It Means to Be Literate: A Disability Materiality Approach to Literacy after Aphasia* is forthcoming from University of Pittsburgh Press.

**Justin Nicholes** is Assistant Professor of Rhetoric and Composition at the University of Wisconsin-Stout. His teaching and research concern the role (creative) writing plays in constructing academic identities, enhancing learning, and supporting college-student persistence. His research has appeared or is forthcoming in *College Composition and Communication*, *Scientific Study of Literature*, *WAC Journal*, *Across the Disciplines*, *Double Helix*, *Journal of Creative Writing Studies*, and elsewhere.

**Carol Rutz** retired from Carleton College in 2017 after thirty years of service. As director of the writing program, she taught undergraduate writing courses, conducted faculty development across the curriculum, and developed a portfolio assessment of student writing. In addition to the *WAC Journal*, she has published in *College Composition and Communication*, *Assessing Writing*, *Peer Review*, *Change*, several edited collections, and with William Condon, Ellen Iverson, Cathryn Manduca, and Gudrun Willett, *Faculty Development and Student Learning: Assessing the Connections* (2016). Currently, she is executive director of the Cannon Valley Elder Collegium, a nonprofit that offers liberal arts courses to senior citizens.

**Christopher Thaiss** is Professor Emeritus of Writing Studies at the University of California, Davis. Author, co-author, or editor of fourteen books, he taught writing in the disciplines and served as the first permanent director of the independent University Writing Program at UC Davis. Before 2006, he taught for thirty years at George Mason University, where he chaired the English Department and directed the writing center, the composition program, and writing across the curriculum. His most recent books are *Writing Science in the 21st Century* (2019) and *A Short History of Writing Instruction*, 4th ed., co-edited with James Murphy (2020).

**Kathleen Daly Weisse** is Director of the Writing Center and Lecturer of English at Marist College in Poughkeepsie, New York. Her research interests include anti-racist writing instruction, critical data studies, and writing across the curriculum. Her work appears in *Rhetoric Review* and *Across the Disciplines*.

**Terry Myers Zawacki** is Associate Professor Emerita of English at George Mason University. She has published on writing in the disciplines, writing assessment, WAC and L2 writing, writing centers, and writing fellows. She serves on the editorial boards of *Across the Disciplines*, the *WAC Journal*, and the WAC Clearinghouse. She also is lead editor of the WAC Clearinghouse International Exchanges on the Study of Writing series.

## SUBSCRIPTIONS

*The WAC Journal* is an open-access, blind, peer-viewed journal published annually by Clemson University, Parlor Press and the WAC Clearinghouse. It is published annually in print by Parlor Press and Clemson University. Digital copies of the journal are simultaneously published at The WAC Clearinghouse in PDF format for free download, http://wac.colostate.edu/journal/. Print subscriptions support the ongoing publication of the journal and make it possible to offer digital copies as open access.

- One year: $25
- Three years: $65
- Five years: $95

You can subscribe to *The WAC Journal* and pay securely by credit card or PayPal online at http://www.parlorpress.com/wacjournal. Or you can send your name, email address, and mailing address along with a check (payable to Parlor Press) to

Parlor Press
3015 Brackenberry Drive
Anderson SC 29621

Subcribe to the
WAC Journal

Clemson University    WAC Clearinghouse

# PARLOR PRESS
## EQUIPMENT FOR LIVING

## Now with Parlor Press!

*Studies in Rhetorics and Feminism*
  Series Editors: Cheryl Glenn and Shirley Wilson Logan

*Emerging Conversations in the Global Humanities*
  Series Editor: Victor E. Taylor

## New Releases

*Rhetorical Listening in Action: A Concept-Tacticc Approach*
  by Krista Ratcliffe and Kyle Jensen

*A Rhetoric of Becoming: USAmerican Women in Qatar*
  by Nancy Small

*Emotions and Affect in Writing Centers* edited by
  Janine Morris and Kelly Concannon

*Writing in the Clouds: Inventing and Composing in
  Internetworked Writing Spaces* by John Logie

## MLA Mina Shaughnessy Prize and CCCC Best Book Award 2021!

*Creole Composition: Academic Writing and Rhetoric in the
  Anglophone Caribbean,* edited by Vivette Milson-Whyte, Raymond
  Oenbring, and Brianne Jaquette

## Check Out Our New Website!

*Discounts, blog, open access titles, instant downloads, and more.*

www.parlorpress.com

*WAC Journal* **Discount:** Use WAC20 at checkout to receive a 20% discount on all titles not on sale through August 1, 2022.

www.ingramcontent.com/pod-product-compliance
Lightning Source LLC
Chambersburg PA
CBHW030410170426
43202CB00010B/1558